INCONVENIENT

HERITAGE

HERITAGE, TOURISM, AND COMMUNITY

Series Editor: Helaine Silverman
University of Illinois at Urbana-Champaign

Heritage, Tourism, and Community is an innovative new book series that seeks to address these interconnected issues from multidisciplinary and inter-disciplinary perspectives. Manuscripts are sought that address heritage and tourism and their relationships to local community, economic development, regional ecology, heritage conservation, and preservation, as well as related indigenous, regional, and national political and cultural issues. Manuscripts, proposals, and letters of inquiry should be submitted to *helaine@uiuc.edu*.

The Tourists Gaze, the Cretans Glance: Archaeology and Tourism on a Greek Island, *Philip Duke*

Coach Fellas: Heritage and Tourism in Ireland, *Kelli Ann Costa*

Inconvenient Heritage: Erasure and Global Tourism in Luang Prabang, *Lynne M. Dearborn & John C. Stallmeyer*

INCONVENIENT HERITAGE

ERASURE AND GLOBAL TOURISM IN LUANG PRABANG

Lynne M. Dearborn

John C. Stallmeyer

Walnut Creek, California

LEFT COAST PRESS, INC.
1630 North Main Street, #400
Walnut Creek, CA 94596
http://www.LCoastPress.com

ISBN 978-1-59874-435-4 hardcover

Library of Congress Cataloguing-in-Publication Data:
Dearborn, Lynne.
    Inconvenient heritage : erasure and global tourism in Luang Prabang / Lynne Dearborn, John C. Stallmeyer.
       p. cm.
    Includes bibliographical references and index.
    ISBN 978-1-59874-435-4 (hardcover : alk. paper)
    1. World Heritage areas—Laos—Louangphrabang. 2. Heritage tourism—Laos—Louangphrabang. 3. Culture and tourism—Laos—Louangphrabang. 4. Cultural property—Protection—Laos—Louangphrabang. 5. Louangphrabang (Laos)—Antiquities. I. Stallmeyer, John C. II. Title.
    DS555.98.L68D43 2010
    338.4'791594--dc22

                          2010002576

Printed in the United States of America

⊚™ The paper used in this publication meets the minimum requirements of American National Standard for Information Sciences—Permanence of Paper for Printed Library Materials, ANSI/NISO Z39.48–1992.

For Our Parents

CONTENTS

LIST OF ILLUSTRATIONS

TABLES

PREFACE

We first arrived in Luang Prabang, Laos, in 2007 as tourists, having spent the previous week in Bangkok at the 10th Conference of the International Association for the Study of Traditional Environments, whose theme that year was Hyper-Tradition. Michael Sorkin's conference keynote addressed the issues inherent in the landscape we were seeing. It is small wonder that we were continually referring to Hyper-Tradition and its manifestations in the built environment of Luang Prabang. By the end of our week there, we had determined that we would have to return soon. This we did the following year.

During this second visit we were not tourists but solidly grounded as architects and urbanists trying to understand how the city had changed since our last visit just twelve months earlier, and also since its designation as a World Heritage Site in 1995. We were able to obtain the UNESCO maps of the city and set about to conduct a postdesignation survey of the entire Zone of Preservation within the Heritage District so as to better understand the factors that determined the nomination, its success, and possible future outcomes. Determined to survey and record the condition of each building in the UNESCO documents, we methodically circulated the peninsula at the confluence of the Khan and Mekong Rivers that makes up the oldest part of

Luang Prabang. We interrupted our survey only to wait out the rain that locals had assured us never happens at that time of year. The result of these structured wanderings and detailed observations and documentation appears in this book.

This is the only book-length treatment of the influence of World Heritage designation on the built environment of Luang Prabang of which we are aware at this date (August 2009). Several beautifully illustrated books on the architecture of the city exist. Of particular note is *Luang Prabang: An Architectural Journey,* whose extensive drawings and photographs are an invaluable resource for those interested in the city's built environment. However, although this particular book raises the question of tourism's effects, it provides no comprehensive discussion of the subject, nor does it provide the reader with the theoretical underpinnings for such a discussion. Our hope is that our book provides a beginning for such a discussion and that it offers the reader a window into the complexities, contradictions, and spatial transformations that result from UNESCO World Heritage designation not only in Luang Prabang but also in the myriad locations where similar transformations are underway.

ACKNOWLEDGMENTS

It is a pleasure to acknowledge those whose assistance made this book possible. We have benefited from the support and encouragement provided by many entities and individuals at the University of Illinois at Urbana-Champaign. First, we would like to acknowledge the support and encouragement provided by the School of Architecture and our colleagues there. We would especially like to acknowledge the school's director, David Chasco, for his continued support of this research. We have also benefited from discussions and participation in various seminars conducted by the Collaborative for Cultural Heritage and Museum Practices (CHAMP), dedicated to the critical study of cultural heritage and museum practices worldwide. We have been fortunate to receive institutional support from the University of Illinois' Center for Advanced Study, The University of Illinois Research Board, and Hewlett International Research Travel Grant Program. Our graduate research assistants, Majd Musa and Fang Xu, provided us invaluable help running down references. Finally, we would like to acknowledge and thank the series editor, Helaine Silverman. From our first conversation about the idea for the book to the final edits, her enthusiasm for the project provided energy and kept us moving on the project.

Lynne M. Dearborn and John C. Stallmeyer

CHAPTER ONE

CULTURAL HERITAGE, THE BUILT ENVIRONMENT, AND WORLD HERITAGE TOURISM

Architecture is a continuing dialogue between generations, which creates an environment across time.
                                            —Vincent Scully (1988)

We shape our buildings; thereafter they shape us.
                                            —Winston Churchill (1943)

INTRODUCTION

The last thirty years have witnessed the unparalleled growth of tourism worldwide. People from all walks of life now travel to seek experiences beyond their daily lives in numbers far exceeding previous eras, when travel was a privilege enjoyed only by the elite. Travel to seek out the unique and extraordinary is fed by the establishment and growth of locations classified

15

as World Heritage. These locations provide a ready source of places "certi-fied" by The United Nations Educational, Scientific and Cultural Organization (UNESCO) as having extraordinary heritage and that are ready for tourists to experience. Cultural heritage, one of UNESCO's classifications of World Heritage, includes "groups of buildings... which, because of their architecture, their homogeneity, or their place in the landscape, are of outstanding universal value from the point of view of history, art, or science" (UNESCO 1972: 2). These building groups can encompass entire city districts, which become World Heritage Cities. Thus a key component of the tourist experience and of World Heritage Cities is the built environment that is consumed as part of the tourist experience but that also is (re)produced as a key component of heritage designation. The intersection of heritage, tourism, the built environment, and World Heritage designation results in a matrix of production, representation, and consumption in which meanings are ascribed by government entities, tourists, and local residents—meanings that may be very different from one another.

In this first chapter we untangle the terms *heritage, tourism, the built envi-ronment*, and *World Heritage* to understand how they relate to and inform the various productions and representations of significance and meaning at tourist sites. Our goal is an understanding of how they become integral parts of the daily experiences of both tourists and local residents of World Heritage Cities. We lay out the case that World Heritage designation relies on the care-ful and measured circumscription and erasure of particular pieces of the built environment. The built environment is not a neutral framework of space. Instead, buildings become meaningful for people as a result of "complex and continuous process[es] of socialization, symbolic interaction, and negotia-tion" (Harrison 2005a: 4). Buildings and the urban fabric they create, when closely and responsively built, provide the setting for daily life. It is through the daily lives and actions of residents and tourists in World Heritage Cities that we begin to understand the influence of erasure and augmentation in the production of meaning.

According to UNESCO, "heritage is our legacy from the past, what we live with today, and what we pass on to future generations" (UNESCO 2009a).

UNESCO believes that cultural heritage and natural heritage are irreplaceable sources of meaning and motivation for the world's people. The initial document recognizing World Heritage and providing for its identification and protection, *The Convention Concerning the Protection of the World Cultural and Natural Heritage* (1972), recognized the need to protect both natural and cultural heritage. As defined by this *Convention*, Natural Heritage included:

- Natural features consisting of physical and biological formations or groups of such formations, which are of outstanding universal value from the aesthetic or scientific point of view;
- Geological and physiographical formations and precisely delineated areas that constitute the habitat of threatened species of animals and plants of outstanding universal value from the point of view of science or conservation;
- Natural sites or precisely delineated natural areas of outstanding universal value from the point of view of science, conservation, or natural beauty. (UNESCO 1972: 2)

Cultural Heritage, in contrast, included:

- Monuments: architectural works, works of monumental sculpture and painting, elements or structures of an archaeological nature, inscriptions, cave dwellings, and combinations of features that are of outstanding universal value from the point of view of history, art, or science;
- Groups of buildings: groups of separate or connected buildings that, because of their architecture, their homogeneity, or their place in the landscape, are of outstanding universal value from the point of view of history, art, or science;
- Sites: works of man or the combined works of nature and man, and areas including archaeological sites, that are of outstanding universal value from the historical, aesthetic, ethnological, or anthropological point of view. (UNESCO 1972: 2)

In 2003, after many years of discussion and study, the General Conference of UNESCO adopted the *Convention for the Safeguarding of the Intangible Cultural Heritage*. This document was put forth in recognition of the many global and local forces threatening intangible heritage that UNESCO and others believe is at the heart of the world's cultural diversity and a guarantee of sustainable development. This *Convention* defines intangible cultural heritage as:

> The practices, representations, expressions, knowledge, skills—as well as the instruments, objects, artefacts and cultural spaces associated therewith—that communities, groups, and, in some cases, individuals recognize as part of their cultural heritage. This intangible cultural heritage, transmitted from generation to generation, is constantly recreated by communities and groups in response to their environment, their interaction with nature and their history, and provides them with a sense of identity and continuity, thus promoting respect for cultural diversity and human creativity. (UNESCO 2003: 2)

The *Convention* goes on to note that "intangible cultural heritage," also known as "living heritage," is usually expressed in oral traditions and expressions, performing arts, social practices, rituals and festive events, knowledge and practices concerning nature and the universe, and traditional craftsmanship (UNESCO 2003: 2). Since 1972, in identifying and protecting examples of natural and cultural heritage of "outstanding universal value," heritage professionals have increasingly recognized that natural and cultural heritage are often interlinked, and their preservation often cannot be considered independently. Likewise, there is now recognition that a "deep-seated interdependence between the intangible cultural heritage and the tangible cultural and natural heritage" (UNESCO 2003: 1) exists and must be recognized in identifying and preserving World Heritage.

CULTURAL HERITAGE

Cultural heritage is intimately linked to works of art and architecture (UNESCO 1972). Ascribing meaning to these inanimate objects allows people to make sense of the past and to make personal connections between their present and the distant past. However, the significance and meaning of heritage in relation to a particular work of art or architecture can vary substantially, because these ascriptions are tied to individuals' background, experience, and socialization. Historically, architecture has been the "gentlemen's profession" and the purview of social elites (Ahrentzen and Anthony 1993). Architects often attribute meanings and significance to buildings that diverge from those ascribed by ordinary citizens. Buildings can evoke strong feelings for both architects and non-architects, not only for their aesthetics but also for the life that has been lived in and around them.

Buildings, particularly historic buildings, can elicit very different responses from architects, preservationists, and ordinary citizens. However, when buildings or groups of buildings become symbolic as representative of a particular heritage and thus worth protecting, the concerns of architects, preservationists, and ordinary citizens must somehow meld into a plan for conservation. Such heritage, although of the past, is connected to a living system, and, in the case study of Luang Prabang presented here, that living system includes the intact rituals, social structures, and daily lives of residents of the numerous villages that make up the city, an intangible cultural heritage. In such a city, the best heritage preservation interventions can hope for is to slow the rate of change, because to freeze the physical environment in some imagined space/time would delink it from its evolving associated living system. Inserting tourism and World Heritage Site status into the process of cultural heritage preservation adds complexity and potential debate to the equation, as added sets of actors influence conservation of the physical infrastructure of architecture and the urban environment.

Heritage and tourism exist in an uneasy relationship. Recently popularized heritage tourism brings this contradiction to the fore. Heritage is central to community formation and identity making (Turtinen 2000). Distinct from the idea of a factual history, heritage "relies on revealed faith rather than rational proof" (Lowenthal 1998: 7). Heritage grows and becomes more useful as a device for solidifying group identity as a result of the fabricated legacy that underpins it. Unlike history, heritage can sanitize the past by selectively forgetting evil or inconceivable acts. Such recrafting of the past in the memory of a people can bring disparate groups together in the act of building local and national identity. Thus heritage functions to define who is part of that identity and who is an outsider. Sites connected to this heritage become revered places to those who take on the associated identity. Heritage tourism, however, puts such heritage on display for others. Through the process of packaging and promoting heritage, important sites become tourist destinations. Designation as heritage adds social significance to buildings, places, and ways of life that may be in danger of disappearing, because their importance has waned under a new world order. "It does this by adding the value of pastness, exhibition, difference, and where possible indigenity" (Kirshenblatt-Gimblett 1995: 370). Through tourism these destinations also gain a new economic value.

Seen in such a way, heritage is local; it offers two types of value to a local population. The first is an identity value, something that can bring a community together, giving it distinctiveness and common purpose. The second is an economic value that can offer new life to a locale that has ceased to be economically viable. Given this local importance of heritage, the idea and the label of World Heritage are not without controversy. World Heritage as defined by UNESCO assumes that there is a "common heritage, reflecting and representing the history of man and nature. . . [suggesting] not nations or ethnic groups as imagined communities, but rather humankind as a moral and imagined community" (Turtinen 2000: 3). Thus world heritage as an idea juxtaposes the needs and the identity of a local population against the needs and the identity of all of humanity.

WHAT IS WORLD HERITAGE?

Lowenthal (1998) describes the use of heritage production by elites as a way to create meaning, gain identity, and establish legitimacy throughout history. The idea of identifying a World Heritage was first considered shortly after the end of World War I (Rakic 2007). The necessity of safeguarding particular sites deemed important to the history of humankind gained the attention of the world and UNESCO in particular in 1954 when the building of the Aswan Dam in Egypt threatened the Abu Simbel and Philae temples. With funding from fifty countries, UNESCO led a successful campaign to have these two temples dismantled and rebuilt on higher ground (UNESCO 2009b).

On the heels of additional successful campaigns to safeguard particular well-known sites deemed universally important, UNESCO adopted *The Convention Concerning the Protection of World Cultural and Natural Heritage*, also known as *The World Heritage Convention*, in 1972. Simply put, this *Convention* identifies "some parts of the world's natural and cultural heritage which are so unique and scientifically important to the world that their conservation and protection for present and future generations is not only a matter of concern for individual nations but for the international community as well" (Slatyer 1983b: 138). Through UNESCO's adoption of this convention, the idea that some heritage has universal value—in other words, is a World Heritage—that surpasses its local and national value was proposed to a world audience. Along with the recognition that some cultural and natural sites embody World Heritage came the commensurate responsibility that all countries of the world have a shared duty to protect this heritage of "outstanding universal value" (UNESCO 1972).

UNESCO

UNESCO and its affiliated expert bodies (that is, ICOMOS, ICCROM, IUCN) constitute several of the important actors operating on a global scale within the field of heritage at the present time. As such, these organizations "are not only guardians of the past but also influential and powerful producers of culture" with the "power to define and diffuse beliefs and practices for cultural and natural heritage" (Turtinen 2000: 3). In addition to providing a means of safeguarding and preserving heritage of outstanding universal value, UNESCO's *World Heritage Convention* was conceived as an instrument "for international cooperation and assistance through exchange of information, sharing of expertise, transfer of resources, and training of experts in the field of conservation" (Slatyer 1983a: 140). *The World Heritage Convention* designates The

World Heritage Committee as the policy and decision-making body. It is composed of a rotating membership of twenty-one of the signatory States Parties to The Convention.

The World Heritage Committee is composed of each member-party's official delegation of specialists for natural and cultural heritage. Conducted at its once-yearly meeting, the business of the Committee is begun early each year by an elected Bureau of seven Committee members. The Bureau carefully considers and makes recommendations to the full Committee concerning nominations to the World Heritage and World Heritage in Danger Lists as well as requests for funding and assistance. The Secretariat, provided by UNESCO, assists the Committee by registering nominations to the World Heritage Lists and requests for assistance, as well as preparing documents for meetings. The Secretariat is also charged with implementing the decisions of the Committee and executing approved requests for specialists to provide preparatory assistance, technical cooperation, emergency assistance, and support for training (Slatyer 1983a).

Once a nomination has been registered by the Secretariat it is transferred to the appropriate international organization of experts (ICOMOS, ICCROM for cultural properties, IUCN for natural properties), who rigorously evaluate whether it meets the criteria for "outstanding universal value" and should be recommended for inscription to the World Heritage List. These expert evaluations are then forwarded to the Bureau, which can make one of three recommendations to the full Committee: inscription, rejection, or deferment requiring more information. At its year-end meeting, the Committee acts on the Bureau's recommendations. Through this process of nomination, evaluation, and decision on inscription, "UNESCO and the expert bodies provide a global 'grammar' with which the dispersed local phenomena can be made sense of, coordinated into, and managed as global heritage" (Turtinen 2000: 5).

Although the process outlined above is presented as impartial by virtue of its highly standardized process and execution by transnational scientific experts, the perspective and criteria applied by UNESCO and its affiliated expert bodies are value-laden, growing from a "western" perspective. These entities decide the terms by which World Heritage is defined and inscribed.

Likewise, the central role of UNESCO and its affiliated experts in this process clearly influences how the world's nation-states frame and preserve local heritage on the world stage. The world's nation-states have much to lose in terms of image and economic and social benefits if their nominations to the World Heritage List are rejected. This power imbalance has been identified and discussed by several authors, including Harrison, who notes:

> In UNESCO-organized activities, "supervision" by experts can sometimes come to mean domination by experts. UNESCO support is valued, prestigious, and important, and in many respects UNESCO sets the agenda. Where, even if mistakenly, it is felt inclusion on the World Heritage List might bring more tourists, and would thus increase economic prosperity and status, it might be considered politic to do what the experts suggest. (Harrison 2005a: 8–9)

The link between inscription of a site on the World Heritage List and potential to increase tourism revenues is not lost on the nation-states that are signatories of The World Heritage Convention. UNESCO World Heritage status brings sites around the world a new level of visibility on the global "Heritagescape" (Di Giovine 2008) with a commensurate increase in tourism.

TOURISM

Tourism is a fixture of modern life for much of the world's population. Tourism, like other forms of recreation, offers diversion from ordinary life. It can enhance one's standing in local society and restore mental and physical health. For all but the most disadvantaged, travel as recreation is an expected part of adult life. Life patterns of elites have long included travel and touring (for example, pilgrimages and the Grand Tour), but, "before the nineteenth century few people outside the upper classes traveled anywhere to see objects for reasons that were unconnected with work or business" (Urry 2002: 5).

The World Tourism Organization defines tourism as the set of activities engaged in by any person temporarily away from their usual environment, for a period of less than twelve months, and for a broad range of leisure, business, religious, health, and personal reasons, excluding the pursuit of remuneration or long-term change of residence (UNWTO 1994: 7). For the purposes of statistics, the World Tourism Organization further distinguishes between international and domestic tourists and between overnight and same-day tourists. The critical defining criteria include a voluntary journey to someplace separate from work and home that is to some degree out of the ordinary, and the return home occurs in a relatively short period of time. In providing the foundation for modern tourism, the Renaissance engendered a desire to seek truth outside the mind and spirit (Graburn 1977). This seeking behavior has been behind the growth of tourism, first among the elite and later among the middle and industrial-working classes. Although tourism has been a part of modern culture since the early twentieth century, it has grown substantially over the last fifty years and has become increasingly international (Urry 2002).

New and improved technologies have progressively stimulated the current internationalization of tourism. The Internet allows people to simultaneously compare broad-ranging destinations, to read reviews by those who have visited, to plan travel, to purchase air flights, and to book lodging and sightseeing trips all before they ever leave home. Likewise, readily available long-haul flights and improved travel technology offer relatively unproblematic access to more locations across the globe. The dramatic time-space compression afforded by technological developments since the close of World War II puts diverse destinations across the globe in competition for tourists. Because tourists are seeking to experience the extraordinary on their journeys, destinations hoping to capture their attention and ultimately their tourist business must represent themselves as having some unique qualities that promise an unusual and delightful vacation from their ordinary workaday life. As Kirshenblatt-Gimblett notes: "It is not in the interest of remote destinations that one arrives in a place indistinguishable from the place one left or from thousands of other destinations competing for market share" (1995: 371). One important way that destinations distinguish themselves from their global competition is through the promotion of heritage. Designation as a World Heritage Site puts a destination in a special world-class heritage category.

Tourist flows are not random but are patterned by information and expectations. For tourists who seek extraordinary cultural heritage experiences, a number of factors influence their choice of destination. As tourism has become a more common phenomenon, cost and ease of connectivity recommend some locations over others (Williams and Zelinsky 1970). Nonetheless, within constraints that various individuals bring to their choices, a range of sites becomes possibilities. It is the construction of a place as extraordinary in promotional literature and in the minds of tourists that makes one place stand out over another. Today many tourists use UNESCO World Heritage Listing as a way of distinguishing which destination will offer the most extraordinary experience. Destinations market themselves as sites of World Heritage and in the process raise the expectations that tourists bring to their travels.

Luang Prabang's reputation as a location that delivers an extraordinary experience is based on its unique architectural heritage. The bracketing and packaging of that heritage becomes a critical component of maintaining its reputation. There is a major incentive to maintain this outstanding example of the fusion of traditional Laotian architecture and Laotian urban structures with those built by the European colonial authorities. It is Luang Prabang's rich architectural and artistic heritage and its special urban development that distinguish it from other locations. Experiencing this unique heritage and the associated culture, and perhaps the nostalgia for a colonial period when life was slower and social lines more distinct, recommend Luang Prabang to tourists from around the world.

WORLD HERITAGE TOURISM

Many conservationists regard *The World Heritage Convention* as a high point of world cultural and natural conservation; nevertheless, it also has substantial significance for tourism (Hall 2001). Securing a place on the List of World Heritage Sites now confers not only worldwide concern for conservation and protection but increasing importance as a tourist destination. In fact, some have suggested that "World Heritage Site status is now perceived as a prestigious acknowledgement of the quality and uniqueness of heritage sites. . . . a reference point for the cultural/heritage tourist, an equivalent of a constantly updated list of 'authentic' heritage sites worth visiting" (Rakic and Chambers 2008: 146).

In his book *The Tourist Gaze,* John Urry focuses on the idea that what tourists seek are sites that offer something extraordinary. Tourists hope to direct their gaze to something that will take them away from what they ordinarily experience in their routine lives. They seek restoration of body and soul by getting away. Urry further notes that "the universal availability of the predominantly visual media in advanced western societies has resulted in a massive upward shift in the level of what is 'ordinary' and hence what people view as 'extraordinary'" (Urry 2002: 92). In this present-day context, The World Heritage List offers a ready inventory of 878 sites in 145 countries that heritage experts have already certified as having "outstanding universal value." Thus, by their listing, World Heritage Sites are distinguished as extraordinary among all possible places that tourists might visit.

An essential element of UNESCO's World Heritage designation process necessarily includes the targeted emending (addition and erasure) of particular pieces of history. The representation of heritage assumes that "elements of the past [that] are presented as heritage. . . have already passed through a complex filtering process whereby someone, or some group, has *selected* them" (Harrison 2005a: 5, emphasis in original). In the process of inscription and representation of World Heritage, these groups include UNESCO-designated heritage experts as well as committees created by the states party. Nevertheless, everything that is presented has arisen from some particular point of view that has bracketed the representation of heritage. Thus, even though UNESCO has put in place requisite stakeholder consultation, the balance of status and power among the numerous stakeholders necessarily involves influences in the process of selection and framing. Conflicts over interpretation of the built environment in heritage tourism as a result of different histories, perspectives, and motivations are not uncommon when different groups are involved. World Heritage nominations are not immune from these controversies and contestations (Harrison 2005b).

respond to local cultural circumstances or for applications in the developing world and in cross-cultural situations (Uzzell 1989a). The accepted professional standards, on the one hand, carry with them a particular Western cultural bias and, on the other hand, can be appropriated to present a particular interpretation of heritage. Some of the more questionable interpretations of heritage actually come from within the heritage industry itself when heritage is used for tourism's commercial value rather than as a part of scholarship and sense of identity (Hewison 1989). This points to another fundamental conflict between heritage and its use as the basis for creating a tourist destination. To create a clarified and unambiguous heritage that can be readily and unproblematically consumed by tourists requires editing of a more complex reading of history through erasure and manufacture.

As in many other cities designated as World Heritage Sites, the potential influx of global tourists and capital to Luang Prabang provided the impetus for the construction of a bracketed heritage defined in part through the built environment. A particular interpretation of Luang Prabang's cultural significance and history by the UNESCO World Heritage Committee in 1995 celebrates the city's "successful fusion of the traditional [Laotian] architectural and urban structures and those of the European colonial rulers of the nineteenth and twentieth centuries. . . [with a] unique townscape. . . remarkably well preserved, illustrating a key stage in the blending of two distinct cultural traditions" (UNESCO 1995). Thus, despite the social and political diversity expressed in the daily lives and actions of Luang Prabang's residents, the justification and thus the management plan for the city are "almost entirely architecturally focused, emphasizing a harmonious blend of indigenous and colonial building styles" (Long and Sweet 2006: 454). Not only does this focus on the physical carefully background the social, political, and cultural fabric of the city, but it also sidesteps a more complex reading of the city's history as the Lao royal capital and romanticizes its period as a French Colonial outpost.

This process of abstracting and bounding history to deliver an image of an uncontested heritage elides the complexities of Laos, ultimately devaluing other histories and heritages but consequently making tourism in Laos easier to package and sell. Thus, although this particular development trajectory for

Luang Prabang serves the needs of a global tourist industry, provides much needed economic development, and serves political needs, the erasures necessitated by this process leave little room for the performance of locally embedded everyday activities and multiple readings of heritage. UNESCO World Heritage Inscription and the ensuing preservation and redevelopment refine and redefine what heritage is in Luang Prabang and freeze the physical environment of the city as an imagined space/time. As this physical environment is increasingly transformed into a display for tourists, its embedded intangible heritage is displaced in space and time.

The broad outlines of this argument concerning erasure are not new in cases in which multiple interpretations of history exist. However, the case of Luang Prabang illuminates three areas that are absent from many other studies and settings. First, it shows the central role of the physical environment or of the erasure of particular parts of the built environment. Second, the case shows how wholesale transformation of the built environment and its accompanying sociocultural landscape can result when several "inconvenient heritages" are systematically or otherwise erased from memory and from space. And third, it illustrates the impact of World Heritage designation on a living landscape that is a place serving as home to a contemporary population, a place where freezing space/time for tourists has a direct influence on the everyday lives of residents.

STRUCTURE OF THE BOOK

In the next chapter we position the case study of Luang Prabang within the context of global tourist destinations as one of many sites of inconvenient heritage. The chapter more fully explores the treatment of inconvenient heritage and the theme of erasure in heritage tourism sites generally and in World Heritage Sites in particular. The cases used here highlight the various ways that erasure is enacted at heritage locations.

Chapter 3 focuses on the historical and geographical contexts of Southeast Asia and the place of Laos and Luang Prabang within the complex history of the region. This chapter links the political and cultural landscape of Laos and Luang Prabang with the spatial.

Chapters 4 and 5 focus specifically on Luang Prabang. Chapter 4 explores the multiple roles that the built environment performs in Luang Prabang: tourist attraction, economic engine, and political unifier. Chapter 5 closely examines the multiple erasures in the landscape of Luang Prabang and attempts to answer questions posed in the first chapter: What in particular has been left out, removed or forgotten? What are the possible motivations for erasure? Who decided what aspects of heritage would be erased, what would be maintained, and what would be augmented?

The final chapter presents a dialogue between the two authors on the themes of global tourism, inconvenient heritage, and the performance and erasure of heritage in Luang Prabang.

CHAPTER TWO

INCONVENIENT HERITAGE

Heritage should not be confused with history. History seeks to convince by truth and succumbs to falsehood. Heritage exaggerates and omits, candidly invents and frankly forgets, and thrives on ignorance and error. Time and hindsight alter history, too. But historians' revisions must conform with accepted tenets of evidence. Heritage is more flexibly emended.

—David Lowenthal (1998)

The production of heritage incorporates flexible emending (both additions and erasures) of events, objects, and actions in order to create a coherent story that insiders will agree to and take on as their own and that outsiders will find palatable. The augmentation and erasure that take place in the production of heritage are sometimes inadvertent and other times carefully considered—and particularly so where contentious or disturbing aspects of heritage are concerned. This chapter focuses on specific examples of the treatment of aspects of heritage that we label inconvenient and how these are treated through the use of emendment.

We identify specific sites where inconvenient heritage, including the unpalatable, incongruent, or politically inexpedient, is effectively erased in social and physical representations. We use this brief treatment of inconvenient heritage to position the case study of this book, Luang Prabang, within the context of global tourist destinations as one of many sites with inconvenient heritage. At Luang Prabang and elsewhere, the emending of heritage, and particularly erasures at various sites with inconvenient aspects in their past, brackets heritage and sidesteps more complex readings and representations of the past. Through this chapter we illustrate that although Luang Prabang is not unique in its bracketing and packaging of heritage, it does represent an instance when numerous erasures of the social and physical structure combine to more radically transform the city than in many other cases.

INCONVENIENT HERITAGE

The past is integral to our sense of identity and allows us to comprehend the present. "Without habit and memory of past experience, no sight or sound would mean anything... objects that lack any familiar elements or configurations remain incomprehensible" (Lowenthal 1986: 39). However, just as individual memories are selective, collective history and, to a greater degree, heritage represent less than the actual past as a result of numerous factors. History is so vast and multifaceted that its recounting cannot hope to be complete and comprehensive or to have a one-to-one correspondence with the actual past. "Three things limit what can be known: the immensity of the past itself, the distinction between past events and accounts of those events, and the inevitability of bias" (Lowenthal 1986: 214). History is further framed in a particular representation of heritage, because heritage is a small subset of history that links to a given group of people in a particular place, at a specific time. Thus heritage must be understood "as a selection from a selection" (Dann and Seaton 2001: 26). In this selection process, heritage promoters must be sensitive to the effects that various heritage representations will have on stakeholders and potential target groups.

Representations of heritage must be acceptable to and resonate with multiple audiences, those whose heritage is being represented, government officials, tourists, and, in the context of World Heritage Sites, UNESCO and its body of experts, to name a few. One of the very difficult aspects of packaging heritage so that it will appeal to tourists seeking a cultural experience is to understand that what might resonate with each different individual is based on one's particular personal, ethnic, and/or national memories and experiences. A number of authors have discussed this issue with respect to the two historic European castles on the coast of Ghana, Elmina, and Cape Coast (Bruner 1996; Essah 2001; Richards 2002). These two castles are part of a group of eleven forts and castles along the coast of West Africa that were inscribed as a group on the UNESCO World Heritage List in 1979 (UNESCO 2009c).

Elmina Castle, built in 1482 as a Portuguese trading post, has a history that includes occupation by the Dutch and eventual sale by the Dutch to the English in 1872. After Ghanaian independence in 1957, Elmina variously housed a secondary school, the government education service, and numerous other government functions, including a police-training academy (Bruner 1996). The Cape Coast Castle, originally built in 1655 as a Swedish fort, was controlled at various times by the Danes (1657), the Dutch, and finally the English (1664), who sold it to the government of Ghana when the country became independent (Essah 2001). These Castles were originally constructed as trading posts where gold and ivory collected by tribal peoples in the interior of the African continent were exchanged for manufactured goods brought by European traders. However, these Castles gained notoriety as major slave trading and transportation nodes during the years of the Atlantic slave trade (until the early 1800s). They housed various functions of the British Colonial administration until Ghana's independence.

The local Ghanaians focus on the long history of the Castles as representative parts of the sweep of Ghanaian history. Different groups of Europeans are specifically interested in the role their nation played in the history of the Castles (for example, the Portuguese church built in Elmina is one of Ghana's oldest

Catholic places of worship). And many African-American tourists focus only on the slave trade, because for them, "the Castles are sacred ground not to be desecrated" (Bruner 1996: 291). Needless to say, the question for the Ghana Tourist Board, along with the local tourism industry, that has an economic interest in tourism marketing is this: What should be emphasized, represented, and interpreted—and to whom? How should these Castles be preserved? If in maintaining the buildings the dungeon walls are whitewashed, the African-American tourist might feel that sacred ground has been desecrated, whereas Ghanaians might feel that this maintenance is necessary to represent the heritage of their government's connection to the buildings (Bruner 1996).

Aspects of the past that are difficult to come to terms with and that cause discomfort among one or more stakeholder groups, such as trade in human slaves, exemplify inconvenient heritage. Heritage that is inconvenient often involves contested claims among rival groups resulting in very different potential spatial outcomes as the cases above illustrate. Although scholars agree that most heritages are contested to some degree, inconvenient heritage incorporates to a greater degree the problems of ownership, control, and representation that are generally inherent in all heritage tourism development. The contested nature of a great deal of heritage results from different interpretations that are linked at points along the length of a historical timeline. In addition, the different associations that groups have had with that heritage and the power hierarchy play an important role in contested heritage.

Sites of contested or "dissonant heritage" (Tunbridge and Ashworth 1996) pose fundamental questions about their possible development:

- Should such sites be commemorated, and for whom?
- What is the purpose of commemoration at these sites?
- In commemoration, what ethical issues must be confronted and resolved?
- Who should control heritage development at controversial sites?
- Whose past should be privileged?
- Is it possible to provide interpretation that embodies all constituent heritages equitably at contested sites?

THE INCONVENIENT IN WORLD HERITAGE

The castles and forts on the Atlantic Coast of Ghana have been labeled *thanatourism* sites as a result of their association with death and suffering as major nodes in the historic Atlantic slave trade (Dann and Seaton 2001). Such thanatourism sites are "rare among World Heritage Sites . . . [because they are] a memorial to infamy and shame rather than a celebration of past glories" (Harrison 2005a: 6). Nevertheless, many sites that become, or are considered for nomination as, World Heritage Sites have inconvenient or contested aspects of their heritage. One such site is Robben Island, which sits adjacent to the Western Cape of South Africa, just over 7 miles from Cape Town across St. Helena Bay.

Robben Island was used as a prison and a place where people were isolated, banished, and exiled from 1600 to 1900 and again from 1961 until the early 1990s. The island has a complex history that has been documented as far back as 1488, when Portuguese explorers landed on the island (Shackley 2001). It was variously a trading post for the Dutch East India Company, a prison and leper colony during part of the 200-plus years of British occupation, and a gun battlement during World War II. In addition to the colonial buildings on the island, it also hosts a number of prominent indigenous and introduced animal and bird species. However, the island is probably best known globally as the location where Nelson Mandela and other political prisoners were incarcerated during South Africa's Apartheid era. One of the primary reasons underlying Robben Island's promotion as a World Heritage Site by the post-Apartheid national government was "related to the desire to built a nation by promoting an integrated heritage" (Shackley 2001: 357). Of course, the development of new cultural tourism products to attract international audiences has economic incentives as well.

As Shackley (2001) indicates, Robben Island's long and diverse history offers many ways to frame its heritage. Some of those "potential futures" address the inconvenient aspects in its history as a place of banishment and human suffering, while others avoid or erase the inconvenient. The exact nature of the presentation of heritage at Robben Island is still under discussion;

however, the nomination did garner enough support and cooperation among the various stakeholders to succeed in the arduous UNESCO World Heritage List inscription process. This is not always the situation, as the case of Levuka, Fiji, demonstrates.

The town of Levuka, located on the island of Ovalau in the Fiji Islands, is situated 2,000 miles northeast of Sydney, Australia, and 1,300 miles north of Auckland, New Zealand. Itinerant traders of European origin founded Levuka in the early nineteenth century as an important node in the China trade and a whaling boat repair station (Harrison 2005b). At the time of the town's founding, the indigenous Fijian population of the island group was composed of warring chiefdoms. At the insistence of the then paramount chief in the island group, Ratu Cakobau, Fiji became a British colony in 1874 with Levuka as its capital. "Even after becoming Fiji's first capital, Levuka continued to be associated with Europeans, their form of government, and their offspring" (Derrick 1953, quoted in Harrison 2005b: 71). The British soon instituted an indenture system as they had in many of their other colonies. Between 1879 and 1916, 61,000 Indians were brought on five-year contracts as coolie labor to work on Fiji's sugarcane plantations then run by various British and Australian concerns (Lal 2000a). Although the indenture system was suspended and all remaining individual contracts cancelled in 1920, many Indians remained as free residents in Fiji, as their indenture contracts allowed. This history underlies the contested nature of many social, political, and geographic aspects of present-day Fiji, where out of a total population of 827,300, 475,739 (56.8 percent) are indigenous Fijians, 313,798 (37.6 percent) are of Indian descent (Indo-Fijians), and 47,734 (5.7 percent) are identified as other, including Europeans and part-Europeans (Fiji Islands Bureau of Statistics 2007). Each of these groups remains culturally and economically distinct, and the groups rarely mix or intermarry (Harrison 2005b).

The census group identified as "other" plays an important role in the contested nature of heritage in Levuka. Even today, a large and somewhat influential group of ethnic Europeans and part-Europeans remains in Levuka despite the British having moved the colonial capital to Suva on the Island of Viti Levu in 1882. In Levuka, tensions between people with any European ancestry and local indigenous Fijians have built up over nearly two centuries of contact and include disputed land claims by indigenous groups and a remnant colonial social hierarchy wherein European ancestry is privileged. Indo-Fijians are not prominent in the local Levuka dispute, but on a national level the animosities between indigenous Fijians and Indo-Fijians underlie the country's political and economic instability.

The Fijian government nominated Levuka to the UNESCO World Heritage List based on its unique fusion of colonial and indigenous environments. The nomination stalled as a result of several factors related to contested racial and social history in Fiji and Levuka and to differing motivations of UNESCO's Bangkok and Paris offices (Harrison 2005b). Expatriate advisers initially proposed Levuka's nomination as a World Heritage Site in 1994, but the groundwork for the nomination and coordination with the local population fell to a new entity, the Levuka Conservation Committee (LCC). Although the LCC included three Levuka government representatives, it was overwhelmingly composed of those from out of town (for example, Ministry officials and the Director of the Fiji Museum from Suva, the General Manager of the Levuka fish cannery, and representatives of the Provincial and District Offices). The initial work of the LCC coincided with UNESCO's 1994 global strategy to include more underrepresented regions in the World Heritage List. Specifically noted at that time was the lack of World Heritage Sites in the Pacific region (UNESCO 1998). Fiji representatives worked with UNESCO's Asia-Pacific office in Bangkok, which had an initiative to link heritage conservation with tourism and development (Harrison 2005b). Through a series of stakeholder workshops, the voices of a few local residents were included, but the process of organizing Levuka's nomination was largely top-down (Harrison 2005b). In the midst of the World Heritage nomination process in 2000, Fiji's military carried out a coup in the name of indigenous Fijian interests, particularly linked to land rights and economic development (Lal 2000b).

The 2000 coup and resulting upheaval at the national level halted the progress of the nomination. Locally, the coup and its focus on indigenous Fijian interests brought new emotion to the old question of who has rights to the land under the town of Levuka. A bigger issue in the case of Levuka, and one that was raised by consultants affiliated with UNESCO's Paris office, is in what way does Levuka represent Fijian heritage? The town's "early association with Europeans, the emergence of a high proportion of mixed-race citizens, and its subsequent lack of development, have together marginalized Levuka within Fiji" (Harrison 2005b: 80). Furthermore, as a result of history and cultural norms regarding the built environment, the local population has differing ways of understanding and referring to heritage, depending on their ancestry as either indigenous Fijians or of European descent (Fisher 2000, cited in Harrison 2005b). For Levuka, the contested nature of its history, which is divided along ethnic lines and linked to a larger contested history of the nation, seems at this point to have permanently halted its inscription as a UNESCO World Heritage Site. Other sites with similarly contested heritage are used in the next sections to further highlight treatments of the inconvenient in packaging sites for heritage tourism.

TREATMENTS OF THE INCONVENIENT

Hewison (1989) indicates that it is the "Heritage Industry," those who interpret and package heritage for tourists, that undermines the value and meaning of heritage for local populations. In packaging heritage for tourists, the industry cleanses the past of things physically incongruent with the preferred interpretation, unpalatable for tourists who seek something extraordinary or potentially politically inexpedient for powerful stakeholders in the heritage process. In the cleansing of the past, particular material objects are valorized, restored, and represented, setting them apart from the rest of the physical world. When the historic built environment is remade for the present, restoration can erase signs of decay, augment the physical environment to increase its romantic appeal, and focus on an idealized image of the past. Such restorations may recall an earlier age of privilege and exploitation without unpacking the baggage of that age and what it means for the present. Although tourists are drawn to places with historic ambience, "decay and wear usually detract from the appeal of antiquity" (Lowenthal 1986: 144) and can conflict with or even cover up the extraordinary.

Individuals and groups of people often endeavor to forget or rid themselves of a destructive or inconvenient history. Lowenthal (1986: 67) points out that "wholesale destruction of a dreaded or oppressive past has marked iconoclastic excesses since time immemorial.... Not only are public monuments effaced, but intellectual elites are slaughtered to make sure that the new order still forgets the old." The destruction of these unpalatable pasts and the effacing of physical environments include both erasure and addition as complementary and inextricably linked components of emendment.

EMENDMENTS TO THE PHYSICALLY INCONGRUENT

Many places around the world that were once considered quaint backwater paradises are re-envisioning themselves as major international business and tourist destinations. Penang, Malaysia, is one such location. Since 1991 it has embarked on a process of "imagineering" its renaissance (Teo 2003) by using themes to guide development. The initial development plan imagined Malaysia's "Silicon Valley" at the south end of Penang Island, and, on the north end, a range of tourism facilities were imagined around the theme "Pearl of the Orient" (Ling and Shaw 2009). However, as the competition among resort destinations in Southeast Asia grew, "Penang increasingly marketed itself as a cultural treasure of Malay, Chinese, Indian, and other heritages waiting to be discovered through food, festivals, and friendly hospitality" (Ling and Shaw 2009: 53). This new focus on cultural heritage tourism eventually turned to the enclave of Georgetown, with its remnants of residential and commercial buildings dating from the British colonial era in the late eighteenth century. In 2008, Malaysia was successful in getting Georgetown inscribed on UNESCO's World Heritage List as an exceptional example of a well-preserved multicultural trading town in East and Southeast Asia that was forged from the exchanges of Malay, Chinese, and Indian cultures and British colonial power. Each of these left its imprint on the town's architecture and urban form, technology, and monumental art (UNESCO 2009c).

Georgetown, with more than 12,000 old buildings and many intact ethnic communities, has seen significant emending of its physical and cultural heritage on the way to this World Heritage inscription. As the World Heritage documents note with respect to Georgetown, Penang has a multi-ethnic history as a British possession and regional trading node of the British Empire (UNESCO 2009c). In 2000, the Penang population of 1,260,000 was 42 percent ethnic Malay, 46 percent ethnic Chinese, and 11 percent ethnic Indian (Socio-Economic & Environmental Research Institute 2002: 5). Georgetown's multicultural heritage is on display in "living festivals, houses of worship, food, handicraft, and peoples' homes" (Teo 2003: 555). Tourists form a comprehensive image of Georgetown by visiting its historic precincts, ethnic enclaves, and areas of adaptive reuse. In packaging Georgetown as an international heritage tourism destination, the Penang Development Corporation (PDC) has emended aspects of the environment that are physically and socially incongruent with the preferred heritage interpretation of this historic town as an urban fabric influenced by Asian and European cultures.

Through mid-2003, the majority of development financing had been targeted to buildings and districts that catered to the international tourists' search for extraordinary examples of Malay, Chinese, Indian, and British-colonial architecture. This situation left residents to wonder at "conservation by the state [that] has made the temples 'too colorful, like a zoo for the gods'" (Teo 2003: 558). Conservation has made the temples clean and bright, and filled them with elaborate decoration and ornament. However, these actions have idealized the religious landscapes, making them unsuitable for locals who no longer visit the temples, because the places have lost their significance. Through additions of colorful paint and rich new ornaments, the government stripped away decay and wear and in the process erased the meaning of the temples in the lives of Penang's Buddhist, Chinese, and Hindu residents. The joss-sticks and offerings are now placed in the temples by caretakers as props that make them congruent with the image that tourists expect (Teo 2003). Acts in the temples have become a performance for tourists, erasing former meaningful acts by devotees.

Restoration and conservation have specifically targeted six areas formed along ethnic lines, since Georgetown's "culture has been molded by the successions of civilizations that arrived and shaped its urban growth" (Mohamed and Mustafa 2003: 143). Although the government has invested in targeted infrastructure improvements, conservation often has come from the private sector, where redevelopment follows opportunity rather than a well-organized plan. One example, The Eastern and Orient Hotel, was restored as elite accommodation. It "welcomes visitors to what life was like for the upper-class British who worked and lived abroad" (Teo 2003: 558). But the adjacent Public Works Department Building remains vacant and rundown, because for-profit developers could not identify a financially viable project for the building. Despite the apparently ad hoc nature of development in Georgetown, the Malaysian government has intervened in other ways to facilitate private sector action. Thus, on 1 January 2000, the government repealed the 1966 Control of Rent Act to make way for more commercially viable buildings in Georgetown (Lee, Lim, and Nor'Aini 2008). Rent control had first been enacted in 1948 during the colonial era to protect tenants from easy evictions, thus addressing social inequity (Mohamed, Ahmad, and Ismail 2001). The drive for heritage tourism has changed that policy.

Repeal of rent control threatened and displaced age-old tenants living in more than 5,000 units of traditional shop houses where residents worked downstairs in family businesses and lived upstairs (Lee, Lim, and Nor'Aini 2008). As tenants vacated these buildings, because they could no longer afford the increasing rents, the private sector gained control. Although the Penang Heritage Trust fought to preserve old buildings for commercial use, the prime commercial nature of the land undermined the livelihood of more than 16,000 households who saw themselves as "outcasts of Penang society" (Teo 2003: 559).

Since 2003, the ad hoc and opportunistic nature of private development in Penang has begun the physical erasure of aging traditional shop houses. Evictions in support of the physical erasure expunge the social structure of the ethnic communities in Penang's Chinatown and Little India creating an "inner city ghost town" for tourists (Chow Kon Yew, cited in Teo 2003: 559) that is devoid of local lived cultures. Through selective appropriation and strategic amplification, the interpretation and packaging of Georgetown's heritage have simplified the complexities of Chinese, Indian, and Malay heritage as well as romanticizing Penang's British colonial past. Thus Penang's history of race, income, and power inequalities is erased from the tourists' view and from the collective memory of Penang's society. Yet such inequalities are unresolved, as the elderly former residents of Georgetown's ethnic neighborhoods lose their connection to their heritage when the fast-paced world of global development drives them out, because their lives and associated physical environments are seen as physically incongruent with contemporary development goals.

Reimagining Things Unpalatable for Tourists

When tourists look to the past and seek out extraordinary heritage tourism experiences, many hope to find "historic atmosphere" that appeals to the image of a nostalgic past re-imagined with a collective amnesia that jettisons uncomfortable social conditions and sordid realities (Dann and Seaton 2001). In the United States, groups seeking historic atmosphere increasingly find it in re-imagined plantations in the American south. Through re-imaging, "these sites of litigious past have been converted into beguiling locales for tourists to flock in admiration" (Buzinde and Santos 2008: 469).

In re-imagining plantations, the tourism industry employs very interesting and somewhat ironic erasures and additions that sanitize the whole unsavory era of American history. Slaves played a critical role in plantation life. From household chores, to building and upkeep of plantation property, to cultivation of cotton, sugar, and rice, to the running of saw mills and other industrial enterprises, plantations could not have existed as viable economic enterprises without the toil and ingenuity of the enslaved. The lives of venerated historical figures, from George Washington, to Thomas Jefferson, to Cyrus McCormick (Mooney 2004), were facilitated by their slave-holdings. However, the dominant historic narrative in the United States has failed to come to terms with this history, and this collective denial is at the heart of the erasure of slavery from plantation heritage (Buzinde 2007).

Many plantations in the south marginalize or physically erase slavery from their environments by tearing down slave quarters, not mentioning slavery on tours, or referring to slaves as servants (Buzinde and Santos 2008). Mooney notes that even in the many cases in which slave quarters exist on plantations open to tourists, the dwellings are augmented, "now preserved as humble yet neat and tidy cottages. Walls are freshly whitewashed, roofs have no holes, and window glass is intact" (Mooney 2004: 51). These representations ignore the realities of slavery in the presentation of plantation landscapes and erase the intricacies of the social structure that allowed slavery to exist. Buzinde and Santos suggest this is because racism is slavery's contemporary counterpart, and although it is part of the past it is present in today's American social order. Anglo-American tourists typically—consciously or unconsciously— avoid this unresolved social issue and prefer a romanticized image of the Old South to one that addresses the troubling and inconvenient heritage of the master-slave relationship. However, the erasure of the heritage of slavery from the collective memory in the United States marginalizes alternative heritages, such as those of African Americans whose lives may still be affected by the heritage of slavery.

REMOVING THE POLITICALLY INEXPEDIENT

Almost no country is immune from inconvenient aspects of heritage associated with atrocities and acts of repression—either having been a perpetrator or a victim. However, the heritage management process generally promotes the dominant or authorized interpretation of such inconvenient or contested heritage and associated sites by obscuring or removing the politically inexpedient (Smith 2007). One unintended outcome of the development of sites connected with inconvenient heritage can be the opening up of old debates and wounds, because these sites often involve questions of historical guilt and blame that resonate in the present. This process can have political ramifications at various scales and even result in litigation, as it has with historically oppressed indigenous groups in the United States, Australia, and New Zealand (Seaton 2001: 122). "Conflicts over the disposition of objects and the management of [heritage] sites and places are part of a wider process in which governments and their agencies confer, withhold or otherwise regulate claims to political and cultural legitimacy" (Smith 2007: 162).

Recognizing the legitimacy of cultural heritage claims has important consequences in wider struggles for equity, particularly for indigenous groups. Native Americans and Aboriginal Australians have engaged in protracted and well-documented struggles with government and other entities over the legitimacy of their cultural heritage claims. At the heart of these struggles are histories of forced removal from their time-honored and sacred landscapes by white settlers and their governments, cultural differences in understandings of the human relationship to geography, and issues of power and political legitimacy. The centuries-old practice of addressing the politically inexpedient both in Australia and the United States has involved numerous erasures, which continue to lead to unaddressed questions of historical guilt and blame in the present.

White settlement began in Australia in the late 1780s following the British loss of their American colonies during the Revolutionary War. Thus, although conflicts between white settlers and indigenous peoples in the Americas date to the early 1600s, in Australia encroachment onto Aboriginal lands was not set in motion until about 1790. Nonetheless, in both countries, the official process of physical erasure of indigenous groups from the broader landscape was initiated in the mid-1800s. The process of physical removal of Native Americans to reservations in the United States and Aboriginal people to stations or reserves in Australia helped white settlers define indigenous groups as alien, which placed them outside the usual rights and privileges of white society. It also opened up vast tracts of land for white settlement; in both countries, these lands included indigenous sacred landscapes and burial sites (Byrne 2003; McGuire 1992). In both countries this history of erasure and subsequent settlement by whites has created sites to which both groups have heritage claims; touristic development of these sites coupled with the contentious history of forced removal underlies heritage disputes related to these sites.

Moreover, archaeological excavations and the subsequent removal to museums of indigenous cultural remains, when coupled with the physical erasure of people from the landscape, have effectively erased indigenous heritage from site and mind in both countries. This also disconnects descendant people from places that have great significance to them. In Australia, this history continues to affect Aboriginal peoples' struggles for recognition and land rights in a dominant cultural framework that emphasizes entitlement to land through present memory and physical evidence of inhabitation (Clarke and Johnston 2003).

Aboriginal burials speak clearly to this issue. In the 1880s, when government policy enforced concentration of Aboriginal populations in stations and small land reserves, Aboriginal communities had small cemeteries on untitled lands. When the government changed its segregation policy to one of assimilation in the 1930s, lands that had formerly been Aboriginal reserves were sold to farmers (Byrne 2003). One result was that Aboriginal families could no longer access burial sites, because they were now located on private property. Although the policy of assimilation dispersed Aboriginal families geographically, Aboriginal people maintained a strong connection to historical burial sites, making great efforts to "return the bodies of the dead for burial in what people regard as their own country, whether traditional or adoptive" (Byrne 2003: 75).

In addition to the erasures identified above, Clarke and Johnston (2003) note that Australia has been slow to recognize heritage connected to social significance, encompassing attachment to place and meanings, and associations built up through history. Thus Aboriginal sacred spaces that were not marked in ways understandable to a Western worldview were rendered invalid (Thorley 2002: 113). These sites, often of intense natural beauty or significance, were in many cases appropriated as part of an Australian national heritage as in the case of Ayers Rock, also known as Uluru by the Anangu people (see Clarke and Johnston 2003). *The Burra Charter*, adopted in 1979 as the Australian ICOMOS charter for the conservation of places of cultural significance and subsequently revised in 1981, 1988, and 1999, attempts to address this issue. Through modifications to the 1964 *Venice Charter, The Burra Charter* provides for the preservation and restoration of heritage places with process guidelines that are practical and useful given the cultural conditions in Australia. The 1999 revisions to *The Burra Charter* seek specifically to "recognize the less tangible aspects of cultural significance including those embodied in the use of heritage places, associations with a place and the meanings that places have for people" (Australian ICOMOS Secretariat 1999: 1) and to involve people who have a strong association with a place in the decision-making process.

The struggle of Aboriginal people for heritage recognition in contested landscapes of Australia has its parallel for Native Americans in the United States. For instance, in the dominant heritage narrative, Mount Rushmore represents the first 150 years of U.S. history with 60-feet-tall sculpted heads of four U.S. presidents (Washington, Jefferson, Lincoln, and Roosevelt), father figures particularly renowned for their contributions to preserving the Republic and expanding its territory (Boime 1991; Pretes 2003). Initially conceived to promote tourism in South Dakota, Mount Rushmore has become a national icon and an important site of national heritage (Pretes 2003).

However, the Lakota tribe in the region calls Mount Rushmore "Six Grandfathers." It is a sacred site for them, and they believe the mountain and surrounding Black Hills are rightfully theirs by federal treaty. The Lakota assert that Mount Rushmore sits on a vast tract of Indian land taken from them; they call it "Four Thieves" (Fenelon 1997). And for them, the carvings represent graffiti on a sacred site much as if a vandal had spray-painted the devil's name across the front of the Vatican (Watkins 2006). Thus the subaltern narrative interprets Mount Rushmore as defacing spirituality to produce a symbol of white American domination.

In the interpretation of Mount Rushmore available at the visitors' center, no mention is made of Lakota heritage connected to the site (Pretes 2003). The dominance of the sculptures and their national appeal erase the meaning of the Lakota sacred place. The lack of any reference to the contested nature of the site coincides with the social structure that leaves the Lakota living in substandard conditions on nearby reservations. The dominant heritage interpretation at Mount Rushmore and the lack of acknowledgment of the site's importance in Lakota heritage erases the fact and memory of the White government's betrayal of its treaties with Native Americans throughout history.

CONCLUSION

The preceding discussions have provided examples of ways that heritage is emended through interpretation and ways that interpretation generally supports the dominant heritage discourse. Such interpretations often leave little room for negotiations of other heritages that might lay claim to a site or offer alternative views of a location's heritage. Erasures in the physical environment often link symbiotically to physical additions. These physical erasure-addition unions in the built environment are particularly effective in removing alternative heritages from collective memory, because physical remnants, whether old or fabricated, provide tangible relics that make heritage claims credible (Lowenthal 1986).

Physical emendment can also erase references to the long-term effects of a hierarchical social structure if that erasure provides a packaging of heritage that resonates with tourists. Such places as Ghana's coastal castles illustrate the difficulty of erasing the remnants of an undesirable historical hierarchy. Such erasures in the case of Ghana's castles make them more palatable to some tourist constituencies but may be an affront to some African Americans for whom these sites and the memory of the slave hierarchy are sacred.

Physical emending may also have the effect of erasing particularly contested or inconvenient aspects of history from collective cultural memory. In the case of plantation tourism, representations of the physical environment that ignore the realities of slaves' lives erase the memory of the relationship of slave to a master and his household, the lowly position of servility, the powerlessness and the often deplorable conditions of existence of a whole group of human beings. In removing references to this aspect of plantation history, the heritage industry devalues the heritage of slaves' descendants and allows all others to sidestep a more complex reading of history that might better allow the United States to come to a collective resolution of this historical period.[1]

---

[1] Handler and Gable's (1997) study of Colonial Williamsburg is directly relevant to this issue. They discuss the shift in the script of this important American site to become historically comprehensive, which is to say, accurate, by inclusion of the "other half" tour showing the population of slave residents in Colonial Williamsburg, who enabled the genteel lifestyle represented in the built environment. The former exclusion of slavery from the Colonial Williamsburg narrative made that site more "palatable" for tourists, predominantly and overwhelmingly white, and less challenging to noble patriotic sentiments. Although the "other half" tour is optional, and not without controversy, including from African-American tourists, it does seek to remediate the former omissions within the Colonial Williamsburg script.

However, packaging plantation life in a cloak of nostalgia makes it more palatable for tourists and more politically expedient for various powerful stakeholders at plantation tourism venues.

The examples in this chapter have shown that heritage in relation to any particular physical setting can be interpreted in many different ways. There are in fact multiple heritages associated with most places. This chapter has attempted to illustrate that although "in most cases tourists like to believe that they are being told the truth about a destination or are getting a taste of what the place is or was about" (Richter 1989: 187), they are in fact experiencing a particular representation of heritage. That representation of heritage often ignores heritages of marginalized groups in favor of a dominant heritage narrative. Few tourists are well enough informed to distinguish the accurate from the inaccurate or to understand what has been erased and what has been augmented. They may not have the background or critical perspective to recognize whose heritage is being represented and whose is being repressed or distorted.

CHAPTER THREE

LAOS: HISTORY AND CONTEXT

The more we know about cultures, about the structure of society in various periods of history in different parts of the world, the better we are able to read their built environment. —Spiro Kostoff (1991)

A country... is not territorial, but ideational.
—Rabindranath Tagore (1939)

CONSTRUCTING LAOS

Contemporary and historical Laos, as well as the city of Luang Prabang, may usefully be regarded as ideational. By this we mean that throughout much of its history the term *Laos* has referred not to a clear and present object able to be apprehended by the senses but rather has referred to an abstract idea of a geographical entity. Through this process of ideation the geographical Laos was constructed, bounded, and given a physical presence. A key element of this process was its intersection with various local, regional, and global empire building projects that were inextricably linked to the construction of imaginary spaces.

Throughout Laos's history, the idea of the physical boundaries of Laos and the position of Luang Prabang, both physically within this geographical space and as a representation of the idea of Laos, were and continue to be powerful ideas for creating Laos and Lao-ness, first for the various regional kingdoms, for the French, then for the Royal Lao Government, and finally for the Lao Peoples Democratic Republic. During each phase of these nation-building exercises, Luang Prabang was an important setting, its built environment becoming both product and producer of identity for the various incarnations of the geographical territory. The built environment, as noted in Chapter One, cannot be separated from the project of bounding a geographical space and naming the enclosed territory. In this bounding process there is a reciprocal relationship among heritage production, "the invention of tradition" (Hobsbawm and Ranger 1983), construction of nation, and the built environment, as these are integrally woven in a complex tapestry.

A comprehensive treatment of Laotian history is well beyond the scope of this book, given its complexity. One part of this complexity is that the history and context of Laos cannot be understood without considering the overlapping history of its contemporary neighbors, Thailand, Vietnam, Burma (today, Myanmar), and Cambodia. This is because the political and geographic boundaries of Laos that we find on the map of present-day Southeast Asia were formed by and in response to events that involved these neighbors. These boundaries ignore the sometimes centuries-old social, political, and cultural divisions of the region.

Here we provide a brief overview to contextualize our arguments about Luang Prabang. This chapter outlines the major strokes of Laotian history, locating Luang Prabang within the broad arc of precolonial, colonial, and postcolonial social, cultural, and political developments in Southeast Asia. The periodization of Laotian history as presented in several book-length treatments of the subject (for example, Evans 2002; Stuart-Fox 1997) and given in Table 3.1 serve as the chapter's starting point.

In each of the periods shown in Table 3.1, the idea of Laos and Lao-ness were continually defined and redefined. Their history forms an important foundation for understanding the ways that Luang Prabang, and in particular its built environment, is used in contemporary Laos as a means of continuing to construct Lao-ness and to provide a connection to a Laotian past.

PRECOLONIAL LAOS

Stuart-Fox points out that the history of modern Laos as a nation-state begins after 1945 with the departure of colonial French administration (Stuart-Fox 1997: 6). However, several earlier historical periods figure in the geographical, political, and cultural configuration of Laos and the meaning of Luang Prabang in this nation-state formation. Thus we begin our history before the arrival of the French.

For centuries before the late 1800s and the colonial involvement of both Britain and France in much of what we now refer to as Southeast Asia, the area that now constitutes the country of Laos and surrounding territories was defined by a variable and shifting political landscape comprising overlapping power centers with their tributary areas acting as subordinate but independent political entities. These are widely referred to by historians of Southeast Asia as Mandalas and Muang, respectively.[1] Wolters describes the

TABLE 3.1   Periodization of Laotian history.

Period	Date	Features
Precolonial	–1893	Variable/Overlapping power centers
Colonial	1893–1945	French domination
Post-1945	1945–1975	Nationalism
Lao PDR	1975–present	Communism

[1] The idea of Mandala as a descriptor for this political system was first introduced by O. W. Wolters in 1982 (see Wolters 1982).

Mandala as a "particular and unstable political situation in a vaguely defin-able geographical area without fixed boundaries and where smaller centers tended to look in all directions for security" (Wolters 1982: 17). It is easy to see how these formations would eventually fall into conflict with European notions of sovereignty during the colonial period. Each Mandala draws into its orbit various Muang. An important feature of this political formation is the ability of the subordinate entities (Muang) to fall within the orbit of more than one Mandala and thus to pay tribute to more than one higher authority.[2] These Mandala-Muang formations can usefully be thought of as a series of overlapping circles of variable size. The principal political divisions of the period and their geographic areas are shown in Figure 3.1. These included the Mandala-Muang formations of Lan Na, Ayudhya, Lan Xang, as well as Cambodia, Burma, and Dai Viet (Viet Nam).

The territory of contemporary Laos overlaps much of Lan Xang, founded in 1353 by Fa Ngum "on the edge of the Lan Na and Sukothai Mandalas" (Evans 2002: 9), with its center in Luang Prabang. Beginning with his con-quest of Muang Sua, Fa Ngum solidified his control over the territories of other Muang, transforming them into the Mandala of Lan Xang (Evans 2002: 9). It was during Fa Ngum's reign that Theravada Buddhism was introduced to Laos. It is also believed that it was Fa Ngum who brought the Pra Bang Buddha from Ankor to Lan Xang to build Theravada Buddhism and serve as the palladial image for his reign. The Pra Bang eventually gave the city of Luang Prabang its name. As the palladial image for the kingdom, the Pra Bang was believed to possess shielding powers, and it therefore served to protect and legitimate the King's rule.

In the early eighteenth century, the mandala of Lan Xang was divided into three separate kingdoms, Luang Prabang, Vientiane, and Champasak—all of which eventually came under the control of the Siamese court. At the divi-sion of Lan Xang, the Pra Bang was moved to Vientiane. In 1778 the Siamese

---

[2]The allusion to orbits and gravitational forces owes to Lieberman's use of the term *solar polity* as a useful metaphor for the Mandala-Muang formation (see Lieberman 2003).

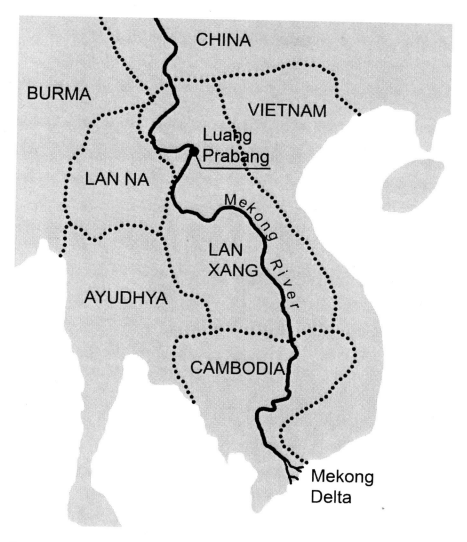

FIGURE 3.1   Mandalas of Southeast Asia (drawn by authors after Martin Stuart-Fox 1997).

removed the Pra Bang to Bangkok after defeating local forces in Vientiane. It was returned to Laos in 1782, subsequently captured again by the Siamese in 1828, and returned again in 1867 to Luang Prabang. Since that time it has been enshrined at The Royal Palace, Wat Visun, Wat Mai, and finally again at the Royal Palace, where it remains today (Center for Southeast Asian Studies 2002). The continued importance of the Pra Bang for contemporary Lao identity and, we may speculate somewhat counterintuitively, the legitimating of the current Lao regime, is evidenced in the construction of a new temple to house the Pra Bang. This new temple is within the grounds of the former Royal Palace, now the National Museum in Luang Prabang. Further evidence of the Pra Bang's sustained importance and of reverence for its power is the continuing prohibition of photographing it—reverence that is not accorded to most other images of the Buddha in Luang Prabang.

By the mid-nineteenth century, the Muang of Laos were all tributaries of Bangkok, with the exception of Luang Prabang, which paid tribute "not only to Bangkok and Hue but to Beijing" (Stuart-Fox 1997: 16). Bangkok was by this point established as the capital of the Kingdom of Siam with the decline of the Ayudhya and Sukhothai Mandalas, and Hue was the center of power for Vietnam, unified by Nguyen Phuc Ahn in the early 1800s.

The French took their place on this stage in the late 1800s. French colonial interests in Vietnam, set in place in August 1883 after a treaty with the court in Hue, exploited the variable geometry of the Mandala-Muang structure to extend colonial control over territory between their Vietnam holdings and the Siamese Kingdom to the west, and consequently Luang Prabang. As Stuart-Fox notes, Vietnamese imperial records that incorporated Lao Muang into the Vietnamese imperial orbit "were a godsend to the French, seeking as they were to extend the narrow confines of their Indochinese territories as far west as possible" (Stuart-Fox 1997: 21). By claiming these Lao Muang as historically Vietnamese holdings, the French began to extend their influence westward toward the Mekong River. The French and the British introduced a new conception of territoriality to the region. As Jerndal and Rigg point out, "the arrival of the British and French and their territorial struggle altered not just the balance of power in the region; it also, and perhaps even more fundamentally, constructed a new spatial 'reality.' For the first time geographical space, delineated by 'lines' of control and ownership (international borders), became of overriding importance" (1999: 36).

THE FRENCH AND LAOS

This expansionist stance taken by France eventually brought it into conflict with Siamese claims to the same territories as a result of the intersecting custody in the overlapping Mandala-Muang geography. Again Jerndal and Rigg note that "Siam's leaders at least had internalized Western concerns for geographical space... [as the Siamese court] had begun to employ cartographers to delimit the extent of the Siamese state" (1999: 36). This French expansion saw the Siamese pressing their position in the late 1800s with respect to their holdings east of the Mekong and in response to the division of Lan Xang into three separate kingdoms. To the north, Siam "tried both bribery and coercion to bring local elite into its fold" (Evans 2002: 36).

The watershed events that solidified French control over Lao Muang territories began in 1892 with the French discussing the dispensation of the territories between Siam and Vietnam with Britain, which held sway in British Burma to the north (Stuart-Fox 1997: 24). The French and British pressured the Siamese, whose failed bribery and coercion were followed by military action in the region. The situation came to a head in 1893 with a piece of gunboat diplomacy on the part of the French, who positioned naval vessels within range of the Siamese palace in Bangkok in response to Siam's attempt to solidify its control over areas of Laos. This action forced the Siamese into accepting French terms for the dispensation of territories along the Mekong.

In October 1893 the Siamese court capitulated to French terms and ceded eastern territories along the Mekong to the French. As Stuart-Fox notes, it was at this time that "French Laos was beginning to take shape" (Stuart-Fox 1997: 25). Over the next fourteen years, France solidified the borders of Laos, culminating in the treaties with Siam of 1904 and 1907, which established the borders of Laos (Savada 1995: xvi). France named Auguste Pavie as first vice consul, with his seat in Luang Prabang in 1887, beginning the French influence on the built environment in the city. Indeed, construction of the royal palace for King Sisavang Vong, whom the French would keep in place, began in 1904. For the next fifty-two years, until 1945, French rule in Laos shaped the culture, politics, and economics of the newly constituted Laos, its borders now more firmly defined than ever before. And in Luang Prabang, the physical transformation began that would eventually bring it to the attention of UNESCO.

POST-1945

In March of 1945, during the waning months of World War II, Japan had occupied Laos and overthrown the French throughout their holdings in Indochina (Evans 2002: 82). The Japanese had compelled the various states formerly under the control of France, including Laos, to declare their independence. Within months however, World War II would end, and the Japanese would leave the scene. With the close of hostilities there began a struggle for power in Laos and much of Southeast Asia that would not conclude until 1975. The complexities of the Cold War and postcolonial, nationalist independence movements, including the relations of local, regional, and international actors, were just beginning to be played out in Southeast Asia, and Laos would find itself at the crossroads of this struggle.

Within Laos three principal factions vied for power: the royalists backing King Sisavang Vong, the neutralists, and the communists. Over the next thirty years, these factions were at various times either aligned with one another in a series of coalition governments or in military conflict as they aligned variously with the United States, France, and Vietnam. Four key figures, all with ties to the royal household, played important roles; three of them were King Sisavang Vong's nephews, Phetsarath Rattanvongsa, his brother Souvanna Phouma, and their half-brother Souphounouvong. The fourth was Prince Boun Oum, of the Princely House of Champassack in southern Laos. As in Lao history before and since, each of these factions had a particular vision of how to govern and to construct Laos and Lao-ness. In the pre-WWII period, the French maintained King Sisavang Vong as the Laotian in power but also placed a French vice consul to guide the country. From 1946 through 1959, King Sisavang Vong was maintained as the King of Laos but with the backing of a range of different political units. Table 3.2 shows the various governments who backed his reign and the subsequent Lao governments.

TABLE 3.2   Reign of Sisavang Vong with government backers.

Years of Reign	Title	Backers of the Regime
Preceded by King Sakkarin		
1904–1945	King of Luang Prabang	French Colonial government
1945–1946	Deposed by Lao Issara	
1946–1947	King of French-controlled Laos	French
1947–1953	King of Laos	Lao Issara
1953–1959	King of Laos	Royal Lao Government/ French/United States
Succeeded by Regent Savang Vatthana		

In the immediate aftermath of World War II, France attempted to reassert its control in the country. From Luang Prabang, King Sisavang Vong concluded a treaty with the French that continued the protectorate of Luang Prabang under the French. Others, however, including Phetsarath Rattanvongsa, were intent on independence from French rule. Phetsarath was founder of the Lao Issara (Free Laos) movement in 1945, whose aim was "to resist any attempt to return to French colonial status" (Savada 1995: xvi). The Lao Issara movement established regional governments in 1945 and deposed the King after he dismissed Phetsarath from the government. For a short time the Lao Issara was aligned with Ho Chi Minh and the Viet Minh. However, under pressure from the French, who continued to retake the country, they were unable to solidify their control or to govern the country in the months that followed. In a last-ditch effort to preserve their control, the Lao Issara government reinstalled King Sisavang Vong in Luang Prabang in 1947. But it was too late to halt the French retaking of the country. In

1946 the provinces of Xaignabouri and Champasak, on the western side of the Mekong, which had been given to Thailand in the Matsuoka-Henry Pact between the Vichy government and Thailand in 1940, were returned to Laos (Savada 1995: 30). This final alteration brought the borders to their present configuration, shown in Figure 3.2. Although short-lived and eventually fading into obscurity as their leaders went into exile in Thailand in 1946, the Lao Issara movement was one of the first important movements for an independent Lao state.

Parallel with these developments, the Pathet Lao, originally known as the Neo Lao Issara and backed by the Viet Minh (who were struggling against the French in Vietnam), gained a foothold in Laos capitalizing on nationalist sentiments. The Pathet Lao were formed in 1950 by Prince Souphanouvong (Phetsarath's half-brother), who had originally been a part of the Lao Issara movement but who had moved toward the Viet Minh after the Lao Issara movement's failure.

In 1953 the French and Lao governments signed a treaty that established the Royal Lao Government (RLG) with King Sisavang Vong named as sovereign of the Kingdom of Laos. In 1959 King Sisavang Vong died, and his son Savang Vatthana succeeded to the throne as regent. Because the country and the region were in political unrest, he was never officially crowned King. The RLG governed with difficulty from Luang Prabang, forming several coalition governments through the 1960s with Souvanna Phouma (Phetsarath's brother) as Prime Minister.

After the defeat of the French in Vietnam in 1954 and their eventual withdrawal from Southeast Asia in 1956, American involvement increased. During the subsequent American Vietnam War, the RLG accepted large aid packages from the United States, which backed the RLG in an attempt to avert a communist takeover by the Pathet Lao. In time, the United States would provide large amounts of aid to the RLG and prosecute a so-called "secret war" in Laos, bombing the Ho Chi Minh Trail that straddled the Laos-Vietnam border. Nevertheless, by the time of the cease-fire agreements between the United States and Hanoi governments in 1973, the Pathet Lao controlled large areas of Laos. The last of the coalition governments, with Souvanna Phouma still at

FIGURE 3.2   Borders of the Lao Peoples Democratic Republic (LPDR) and its immediate neighbors (drawn by authors).

the helm, fell soon after Saigon in 1975, as Pathet Lao forces took the capital of Vientiane. The Crown Prince abdicated in November of 1975, and the Lao

Peoples Democratic Republic (LPDR) was established with Souphanouvong as its first president.

THE LAO PEOPLES DEMOCRATIC REPUBLIC

With the establishment of the LPDR, the new communist government set about solidifying their hold on power and transforming the economy, putting "in place all the trappings of a tightly controlled communist society" (Evans 2002: 176). Many Lao who did not support the new communist government fled the country in the first years of the communist regime, including many of the Hmong ethnic group who had continued to wage battles against the communists until 1977. According to some estimates, 10 percent of the Lao population had fled the country by 1980 (Evans 2002: 178). These refugees included many of the people who were the most highly skilled and educated of the country. This left the new government wanting for skilled administrators both within the government and in the economy.

The government also established "seminar camps" and sent to these camps former government officials and many others who were seen as threats to the regime. It was to one of these camps that the Crown Prince, his wife and son were sent from Luang Prabang in 1977. They are believed to have died there in the early 1980s, although no official notice has ever been made of this.

From its inception, the LPDR faced a difficult task in realigning the economy within a socialist framework. It was further handicapped by the exodus of knowledgeable experts and government bureaucrats. The new government was highly dependent on external aid from the Soviet Union. This dependency was to prove decisive. Even as early as 1985, there was conflict on how to proceed with the economy (Stuart-Fox 1997). The country's leader, Kayson Phomvihan, in several speeches, indicated a struggle between those who wanted to introduce economic reforms and those who wanted to continue the socialist economic policies more rigorously. This led to the market reforms that recast national development beginning in the mid-1980s. Referred to as *Chin Thanakaan Mai* (New Thinking), or the New Economic Mechanism, these new policies brought a realignment and opening up of the economy, and much needed foreign investment (Rigg 2005: 20). The fall of the Soviet Union and commensurate curtailment of its aid to the Lao government solidified these reforms. One consequence of the reforms was the reintroduction of tourists to the country who could provide a source of much-needed hard currency. The increase of tourism eventually brought attention to Luang Prabang and its remarkable state of preservation, and in 1995 the city was designated a World Heritage City.

LUANG PRABANG AS A WORLD HERITAGE SITE

There are numerous contested and contentious points in the precolonial, colonial, and postcolonial histories of the geographic area now called Laos. We have highlighted aspects of these histories that may be considered inconvenient by the current Lao government and segments of the country's population, as well as by tourists from countries who formerly exerted influence in Laos. The framework of emendment that we introduced in Chapter Two is a way to highlight the various treatments of these inconvenient histories in the packaging of Luang Prabang as a World Heritage tourism destination. Tourism in a country like Laos, where a majority of the population has little discretionary income, is—of necessity—targeted to international visitors. Thus, in packaging cultural-heritage-tourist destinations in Laos, multiple parties must agree on a representation of heritage that is believable but that also respects the social, political, and economic needs of the present in Laos. In Luang Prabang these parties include the heritage industry (in this case the LPDR government as a states party), UNESCO-affiliated consultants, and UNESCO's World Heritage Committee. As with the cases of inconvenient heritage discussed in Chapter Two, the packaging of Luang Prabang's heritage as World Heritage requires careful interpretation to create a coherent story that insiders can agree to and take on as their own and that appeals to outsiders.

Since its listing as a World Heritage site, the city of Luang Prabang has undergone a remarkable transformation as thousands of tourists now visit the small peninsula that contains the UNESCO Zone of Preservation. And the rest of Laos, too, has seen the influence of tourists with the Champasak cultural landscape also gaining inscription on the World Heritage List in 2001. Tourists bring their own meanings and motivations with them on their individual visits. Collectively they help transform Luang Prabang and its meanings, as Laos once again undertakes a period of self-definition—this time not with respect to regional power centers or Cold War adversaries but instead with respect to a global tourist marketplace.

The history of Laos, beginning with its inception as the Kingdom of Lan Xang and culminating in the establishment of the LPDR, has been in many respects an exercise in defining something that does not exist "on the ground," that is ideational above all else. Luang Prabang has played a role in this history by providing one of the settings in which the various enactments of kingdom, colony, and nation-state have played out. Its physical landscapes have been imbued with meaning by various regimes and inhabitants throughout this history. These meanings are a critical piece of the history-heritage-built-environment matrix that is now represented in the tourist landscape of Luang Prabang. In the next chapters we turn to this tourist landscape and focus on the emendment that is both process and product of contemporary Luang Prabang.

CHAPTER FOUR

THE BUILT ENVIRONMENT OF LUANG PRABANG

By means of its storage facilities (buildings, vaults, archives, monuments, tablets, books), the city became capable of transmitting a complex culture from generation to generation, for it marshaled together not only the physical means but the human agents needed to pass on and enlarge this heritage.
—Lewis Mumford (1989)

LUANG PRABANG: A GEOGRAPHY

This chapter outlines aspects of the physical framework that undergird the life of Luang Prabang's residents and perform as a tourist landscape. This framework includes both the natural geography and the built environment. Although our focus is on the latter, the natural geography is an important starting point, because it informs many aspects of Luang Prabang's urban form. We also include some discussion of the connection between these physical frameworks and the social life of residents at various scales from the region to the village and to the household level. The chapter is divided into two parts: the first part outlines the physical features of the city, including its natural setting and elements of its built environment; the second part then looks at how the UNESCO-mandated preservation plan, as prepared under the aegis of La Maison du Patrimoine, treats these various elements. Our goal is to highlight the variety of the built environments in the city and the various roles they play, and to contrast this with the bracketed physical history that is considered under the preservation plan as important in "preserving" Luang Prabang.

As architects and urbanists we take a broad view of what elements of the landscape have value. Therefore, the purpose of this chapter is to point out the diversity of features, especially architecture and its associated social life, and to consider those features that have been elevated to special status within the World Heritage documents. We do this as a prelude to and a way to a better understanding of the process of emendment that is explicated in Chapter Five.

The Mekong and the Nam Khan

The most important feature of Luang Prabang's physical geography is the Mekong River. The confluence of the Mekong and the Nam Khan Rivers generates the peninsula that forms the heart of the city and its rhythms. The map in Figure 4.1 shows the general geographical layout of the region of Luang Prabang.

What is evident here is the unique geography of the city's setting. First, the city's location at the confluence of the Nam Khan and Mekong Rivers provides unique vistas onto both rivers and the hillsides and mountains that rise from their flood plains. From several locations in the city one is able to survey a vast area of the surrounding landscape. Second, this location afforded a ready means of transport, limited by the Mekong's unnavigable stretches but nevertheless providing at least regional connections via the several navigable tributaries of the Mekong to the north and the Nam Khan River itself.

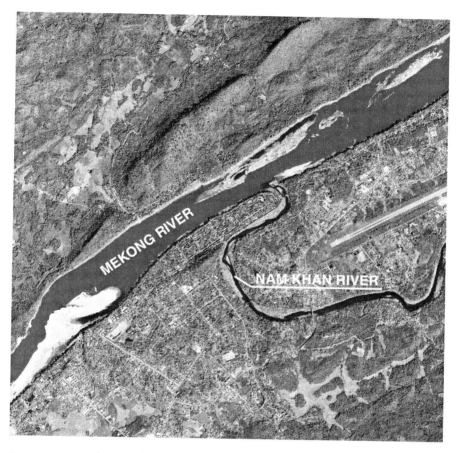

Figure 4.1   Luang Prabang region (contains material copyright Digitalglobe, LLC).

The final defining feature of the peninsula is Mount Phousi, which rises in its middle to a height of 150 meters. Topped by the That Chomsi Stupa, Mount Phousi is visible from nearly all locations within the city and from a distance beyond.

URBAN MORPHOLOGY AND GROWTH

Luang Prabang began to develop as villages grew up around the wat (temple) complexes that were established on the peninsula. Sixteen of these villages are located wholly or partly within Luang Prabang's Heritage Preservation Zone. With their boundaries delineated on UNESCO documents, and each with its own elected headman, the villages are recognized political entities with their own social and political orders. With varying sizes and shapes, as can be seen in Figure 4.2, almost all have access to either the Mekong River or the Nam Khan River. Neither the villages' physical boundaries (Figure 4.2) nor their social structures are readily apparent on the ground. However, an understanding of them is important to comprehend the role of the village structure and physical environment in the daily lives of Luang Prabang's residents and their transformation under the influence of contemporary tourism.

The original pattern of the villages was non-orthogonal. Houses were "clustered around the compound of the leading aristocrats" (Dick and Rimmer 1998: 2307)—in this case the King—and oriented with respect to their relationship with the river and other physical/geomantic attributes of the site. Houses were typically oriented with their long axes parallel to the river in a generally north-south direction.

This individual village morphology, where the wat is the center of each village, and the relationship of the villages to one another, where there is no urban core among the several grouped villages, form Luang Prabang's unique urban structure. This is "an ancient Tai settlement pattern known elsewhere only from archaeological remains" (UNESCO 2004: 23). In Luang Prabang, tourists can experience this pattern as well as the unusual geography of Luang Prabang's peninsula, which condenses this settlement pattern of clustered small villages into a tight array of urban fabric where the wats of each village become a prominent defining feature of the urban landscape.

Historically, these villages existed in a symbiotic relationship in which each village produced a specialty item, such as rice crackers, woven textiles, or pottery, which it supplied to the surrounding villages. The making and trading of these products in the villages is an essential component of the immaterial environments of the city as it now exists. This work generally takes place either at the household level or at the extended family level. Figure 4.3 shows an example of cooperative production of flat rice crackers by an extended family group on a porch in *Ban* (village) *Phoneheuang*. For the most part, these home

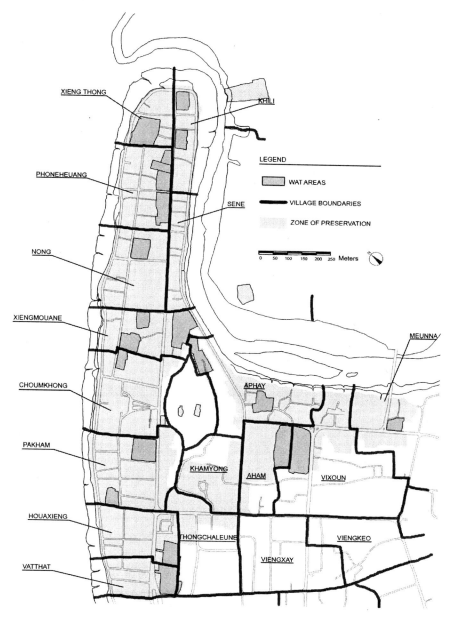

FIGURE 4.2   Villages of Luang Prabang and their wat complexes (drawn by authors).

FIGURE 4.3   Ban Phoneheuang (photo by authors).

industries do not exist to cater to the tourist trade but rather are an integral part of the historic reciprocal social relationships among villages. Likewise, the extended family structure, which underlies these home industries, is fundamental to the social and political structure of the villages.

Lao kinship ties historically linked all village members and allowed the village to function as a social and political unit. Extended-family ties linking villagers were reinforced by reciprocal labor exchanges, participation in village political councils, vested interests in the local temple, and village ceremonies to honor common ancestral spirits (LeBar and Suddard 1967). Although the communist party attempted to alter these centuries-old structures when they came to power in 1975, their efforts were largely unsuccessful in the long term, and the Lao household remains a nuclear family that acts as an economic unit where all productive property and family labor combine for collective use and mutual gain. The strength of village social fabric therefore remains based on reciprocal ties of extended families and connection to the village wat (Rehbein

2007; UNESCO 2004). More recently, "even committed communists now talk of the need to inculcate Buddhist moral values, and the Party is providing funding for Buddhist monasteries to mount courses of moral instruction for the young" (Stuart-Fox 1996: 243). Nonetheless, as we will see, this sociocultural framework is under considerable stress in Luang Prabang from the influence of global tourism (Rehbein 2007; UNESCO 2004).

Like colonialism in other cities, the French period of colonialism in Luang Prabang brought new urban forms and building types to the city. A lasting change was brought by the superimposition of an orthogonal grid of streets onto the village landscape of the city. A main north-south street down the center of the peninsula was introduced, and later in the early 1900s a perpendicular one leading east reorganized the villages along the street frontages created by these and other secondary streets (Atelier de la Péninsule 2004). Shop houses began to line the street frontage of blocks, leaving the interior of blocks relatively unaffected. This general form has persisted until the present with almost no changes in the organization of blocks in the zone of preservation. The wats and evolving house forms continued to define the built environment of the villages. The texture and grain of this urban fabric is made up of a manifold of streets, lanes, and buildings that together serve to create the framework for the social life of the village, and collectively the city as a whole. This framework represents the unique fusion of indigenous and colonial forms. As the UNESCO documents state, this fusion is one of the extraordinary features of the city's urban fabric.

THE WAT

The centerpiece of each village is its Buddhist temple, or wat, compound, which is primarily supported by the village members and is the religious, cultural, educational, and social center of each village (UNESCO 2004). Although the many wats (Figure 4.2) are a highly visible element of Luang Prabang, as are the saffron-robed monks who inhabit them, the central role of the buildings and the monks in the social and cultural life of the villages may not be readily apparent to tourists. Theravada Buddhism, key to the spiritual well-being of most Laotians and the dominant and official faith of Laos, provides an underpinning for Lao society that is deeply embedded in the physical landscape of Luang Prabang. The monks (the local Buddhist clergy for each village) are fixtures of the temple compounds, such as the one shown in Figure 4.4. Each wat complex contains a temple for lay worshippers, a sacred temple for monks, libraries, votive shrines, dormitories, guesthouses, and reception halls.

Historically, these complexes played a critical role in the village, providing a link between the spiritual and temporal worlds of the village. The monks who reside at these wats are a ubiquitous feature of contemporary Luang Prabang and continue to be the embodiment of Theravada Buddhism in the individual villages. The monks of each wat, collectively known as the Sangha, continue to be responsible in part for village education and form an important social and cultural support system for the village. In return, villagers, demonstrating humbleness and respect, provide for wat maintenance and support the wat and its monks with daily alms. In addition, most young men spend at least some time as a novice monk in their local wat. From their vantage point on the peninsula, the wats occupy a prominent symbolic and physical position within the blocks of the city that surround them. These blocks variously contain housing and commercial and institutional structures of different types and in a range of mixes dependent on their location in the city.

HOUSING

The vast majority of Luang Prabang's built environment consists of housing. Just as the larger structure of the city has evolved over the centuries as a result of the Laotian and French Colonial influences, so too has the residential fabric of the city. Thus, there are many variations in form and materials, depending on age, influence, and original ownership of the structure.

First, the Lao house has several distinct features that are notable. (We speak of the Lao house in this context as referring to the lowland Lao as opposed to the many ethnic groups whose house forms reflect their own particular

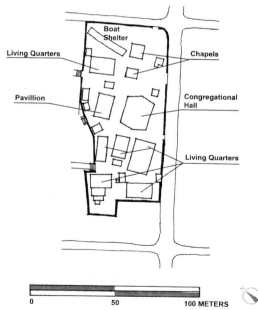

FIGURE 4.4   Typical wat complex plan and temple (plan drawn by authors, photo by
authors).

sociocultural perspectives and worldviews.) As the primary original inhabitants of the villages now constituting Luang Prabang, it is the Lao whose influence is felt most strongly in the residential vernacular. These houses, made
originally from wood and bamboo and raised on piles, are similar to the vernacular Lao houses historically in place throughout the region (UNESCO
2004). The features of these houses are interwoven with the belief system of
the Lao, which is based in part in both Theravada Buddhism and an animist
belief system (see Long 2003).

The house in Figure 4.5, located on the main street in Luang Prabang,
shows several of the features of the Lao house, notably the single gable running
the length of the house and upper story veranda that runs the length of the living space on this level, as well as the stair from the ground level that provides
access to the veranda. As an example of the underlying physical framework
noted earlier, this single main gable is oriented on a north-south axis parallel

FIGURE 4.5   Lao wooden house with veranda (photo by authors).

to the Mekong. Built of a timber frame with infill of wood, the house's living quarters are on the upper story. The lower level, which is many times left open, provides space for work and storage as well as lifting the living quarters above any flood danger and allowing the passage of cooling breezes beneath the living space. In the background, and visible to the right, is the smaller gable running perpendicular to the main gable. This separate structure houses the food preparation areas in this house form.

The arrival of the French in Laos and Luang Prabang brought not only a shift in the layout of individual blocks, owing to the superimposition of a street grid, as mentioned earlier, but also new materials and forms to the housing built in the city. The French introduced two new materials to residential construction in Luang Prabang, brick and torchis (a technique using plaster and straw on a woven bamboo substructure, similar to wattle and daub). These materials were combined with the wood forms already prevalent in the city, yielding several hybrid types with variously brick or torchis bases and wooden upper floors or entire houses of brick or torchis. These hybrid types retained many of the formal characteristics of the indigenous houses including gables and detached kitchens. Figure 4.6 shows a house with a torchis base and a wooden upper story that retains the basic formal geometry of the Lao house. Wood, brick, and torchis materials were used in several other arrangements, including a double gable form as well as a form in which the separate kitchen is eliminated.

The French influence on housing form is also evident in the fully plastered house, such as the one shown in Figure 4.7. This house also illustrates the inclusion of a more formal "French stair" as opposed to a ladder stair (Figure 4.5). This stair, used to access the main living floor, is one of the most important formal additions brought about by French influence. The resulting hybrid houses, like the example in Figure 4.7, give the appearance of being much more substantial structures than do the traditional Lao houses (Figure 4.5).

The French building style and detailing continued to influence Laotian residential architecture and inspired the development of more heavily French-influenced houses, popular among the Laotian aristocracy around the beginning of the twentieth century. The house in Figure 4.8 shows one such building.

FIGURE 4.6   French-influenced house (photo by authors).

FIGURE 4.7   House with "French stair" (photo by authors).

FIGURE 4.8   French-inspired mansion of Laotian Aristocracy; today it is the Villa Santi Hotel (photo by authors).

Formerly a royal mansion and home of members of the extended royal family, this building now houses a popular upscale hotel within the Zone of Preservation.

THE CONCRETE MODERN

Aside from these historic house forms there are also, scattered throughout the city, a number of what, for lack of a better term, we call "concrete modern." These houses typically have lower roof pitches and formal arrangements that do not align with the traditional house forms and are constructed with concrete structural and wall systems. The house in Figure 4.9 is a good example of this type. It is often difficult to discern when these houses may have been constructed; however, most predate the 1995 World Heritage designation. Such construction has been forbidden since the official adoption of the preservation regulations in 2001. These regulations are discussed in detail later in this chapter.

FIGURE 4.9   Concrete modern residence (photo by authors).

COMMERCIAL BUILDINGS

In addition to these housing types that form the greatest share of the land-scape, there are a number of commercial buildings that predominantly line blocks adjacent to the main street. These spaces, as noted earlier, were originally developed as a result of the orthogonal grid of streets imposed on the village layout by the French. These buildings, like the houses discussed above, take several forms. The first is a traditional form seen in many towns and cities throughout Southeast Asia and is inspired by the shop houses of Chinese merchants. Many of the Chinese-style shop houses found in Luang Prabang were built by skilled Vietnamese laborers brought to the city by the French to execute French public works (UNESCO 2004). These shop houses combine commercial space on the ground floor with living space above or behind the shop area. As shown in Figures 4.10 and 4.11, these hybrid commercial structures line many of the main streets through the peninsula.

FIGURE 4.10   Chinese-style shop houses along Sakkaline Road (photo by authors).

FIGURE 4.11   Shop houses along Sakkaline Road (photo by authors).

In addition to the Chinese-style shop houses that historically brought commercial and living spaces together in one building, residential structures throughout the city are increasingly accommodating small shops in one or more rooms on the ground floor while continuing to serve as a family residence in the rest of the house.

Another example that illustrates the ad hoc nature of commercial development in some parts of the zone of preservation, Figure 4.12 captures a scene along the main road in the concentrated tourist zone. This photograph shows at once three different types of commercial construction in this area. The first commercial structure on the right was still under construction at the time of our survey. It employs the relatively standard concrete structural system with brick infill and has relatively large window openings on the ground floor. The ground floor is also set very close to street level, without veranda or transition space between sidewalk and shop interior. The second commercial structure

Figure 4.12 Commercial mix in main tourist area (photo by authors).

sits behind the umbrella in the center of the photograph. This relatively open-air and somewhat temporary structure holds the Khmu Restaurant and behind, in the interior of the block, the Khmu Massage Spa. On the left, a three-story concrete building of a more modernist form houses a popular small café on the first two levels.

INSTITUTIONAL BUILDINGS

Institutional buildings and uses dominate a number of blocks of the city. Like the housing and the commercial buildings discussed above, these institutional buildings take a variety of forms. Many of these structures, like those shown in Figures 4.13 and 4.14, illustrate the French colonial administrative buildings constructed as the French assumed political and administrative control of Laos (UNESCO 2004). Such structures include the former Customs House

FIGURE 4.13   Former customs house, now La Maison du Patrimoine (photo by authors).

FIGURE 4.14   Lao-French Cultural Center (photo by authors).

(now La Maison du Patrimoine, or Heritage House), shown in Figure 4.13, and represent the colonial style that the French developed in Vietnam. As a result, these buildings are better suited to the Laotian climate than true European styles would be. Many of these colonial administrative buildings have been renovated and now house Lao governmental functions, while others house a range of institutional uses.

THE PSMV DESIGNATIONS AND CATEGORIZATIONS: VALORIZING COLONIAL BUILDINGS

As with all sites designated as World Heritage Sites by UNESCO, the preparation of a plan for preservation in Luang Prabang took place under the aegis of local state authorities. This plan is then administered by these same local state authorities. In the case of Luang Prabang, the local authority is La Maison du Patrimoine, which published the *Plan de Sauvegarde et de Mise en*

Valeur (PSMV), The Heritage Preservation and Development Master Plan for Luang Prabang, in 2001. Of the several volumes that make up the PSMV, the most important for our purposes are the *Reglement* (Regulation), the various *Fascicule de Recommandation*, or Reference Manuals, and the Building Inventories. These three volumes, along with several others, regulate all aspects of construction for the preservation of existing buildings and the construction of new structures within the variously defined zones of protection and preservation. Administratively, La Maison du Patrimoine controls the licensure of "all works prone to modify land plot status, public or private, with or without construction" (La Maison du Patrimoine 2001: 3).

Like the measuring and categorizing undertaken by the French Colonial project, the preservation plan for Luang Prabang efficiently places buildings into several categories. How the buildings have been categorized is dependent on their perceived contribution to the World Heritage designation, which as noted earlier, has as its goal the preservation of the unique combination of colonial and Lao building types and urban forms. The PSMV Regulation defines both the boundaries within which several sets of regulations apply and the regulations themselves. This exhaustive eighty-one-page document covers all aspects of the built environment from building materials to lot coverage, building volumes, and signage. The boundaries of the various preservation zones are shown in Figure 4.15 and include the Zone of Preservation (ZPP-Ua), the Zone of Protection (ZPP-Ub), and the Zone of Nature and Scenery (ZPP-N). The remainder of this chapter concerns the ZPP-Ua, which encompasses the peninsula of the city and extends southeast to Ban Meunna near the bridge over the Nam Khan River.

To understand how emendments within the ZPP-Ua affect the built environment, one must understand how buildings within this zone are placed in the various categories created by the PSMV Regulation. The detailed map of the ZPP-Ua in Figure 4.16 shows the boundary and extents of the ZPP-Ua, the buildings that fall within it, and their various categorizations as defined in the PSMV.

Table 4.1 details the building classifications and regulations noted in the *Luang Prabang World Heritage City of UNESCO, PSMV Heritage Preservation*

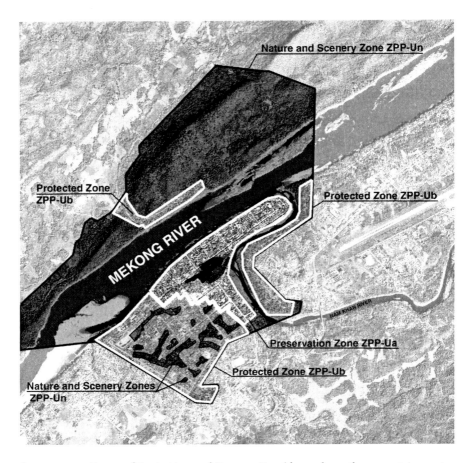

FIGURE 4.15   Zones of Protection and Preservation (drawn by authors, contains material copyright Digitalglobe, LLC).

and Development Master Plan. Three distinct classifications are used: (1) buildings included in the inventory of the PSMV; (2) buildings not included in the inventory; and (3) archeological vestiges that are beyond the scope of this discussion. The first two classes are further subdivided, yielding five subcategories.

The Regulation of the PSMV circumscribes a detailed set of rules and instructions that are applicable to the buildings in the categories of Table 4.1.

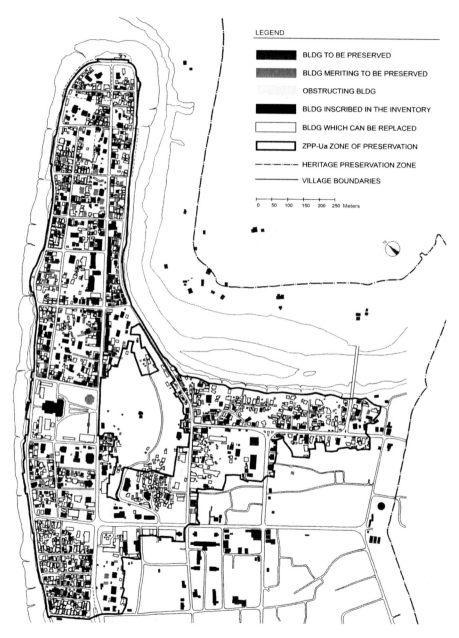

LEGEND

BLDG TO BE PRESERVED

BLDG MERITING TO BE PRESERVED

OBSTRUCTING BLDG

BLDG INSCRIBED IN THE INVENTORY

BLDG WHICH CAN BE REPLACED

ZPP-Ua ZONE OF PRESERVATION

HERITAGE PRESERVATION ZONE

VILLAGE BOUNDARIES

0   50   100   150   200   250 Meters

FIGURE 4.16   Map of Luang Prabang Zone of Preservation (drawn by the authors from satellite imagery and UNESCO data).

Table 4.1   PSMV building classifications.

Classification	Subcategories	Color Coding in PSMV
1. Buildings included in the inventory of the PSMV	Buildings of the inventory constitutive of the dossier of the presentation of Luang Prabang to UNESCO	BLACK *(black in Fig. 4.16)*
	Buildings to be preserved and restored	RED *(dark gray)*
2. Buildings not included in the inventory of the PSMV	Buildings worth[y] of being preserved and restored	ORANGE *(med. gray)*
	Buildings that can be replaced	WHITE *(white)*
	Buildings perturbing the landscape	YELLOW *(light gray)*
3. Archeological vestige		

The first classification is divided into two subcategories, the first of which encompasses those buildings that were used as part of the nomination of Luang Prabang for World Heritage status. These are indicated in black on all maps in the PSMV and are subject to the most stringent UNESCO requirements. Black-coded buildings receive the most stringent guidelines in the PSMV. It states that "rehabilitation work to keep to original, possibility for evolution to be determined case by case, on consent of La Maison du Patrimoine. Demolition prohibited. In case of demolition by accident or malevolence, reconstruction to keep identical to original" (La Maison du Patrimoine 2001: 15). Buildings in this category are located throughout the zone of protection and include wats, houses of many types, commercial buildings, and colonial institutional buildings.

The second subcategory encompasses buildings included in the PSMV inventory but that were not part of the UNESCO nomination documents. These are coded red in the PSMV and dark gray in Figure 4.16. These buildings are subject to the same set of guidelines as the "black-coded" buildings. These two subcategories represent the exemplars. They are used to define the typologies to be applied to and followed in reconstruction or new construction. These typologies are defined in terms of roof pitches, materials, colors, and physical relationships with roads and surroundings.

The second classification encompasses buildings not included in the inventory of the PSMV—in other words, all other buildings within the zone of protection. These are divided into three additional subcategories. Buildings in the first of these subcategories are coded in orange, medium gray in Figure 4.16, and are deemed "buildings worth[y] of being preserved and restored" (La Maison du Patrimoine 2001: 15). The provisions for their preservation and/ or restoration are given in the PSMV as follows: "In case of preservation or transformation, the works should be conceived in reference to the constructive mode and concerned typology. Extensions will be authorized in reference to articles of the regulation relating to the density, coverage, and height authorized. In case of reconstruction, respect of original typology and volumetry" (La Maison du Patrimoine 2001: 15).

The second subcategory of buildings not included in the PSMV inventory is called buildings that can be replaced. These are coded as white in the PSMV and map in Figure 4.16. The regulation for these reads: "Rehabilitation of these constructions can be submitted to the respect of the architectural prescriptions in respect of their own typology. In case of reconstruction, application of the rules relating to construction possibility and architectural prescription" (La Maison du Patrimoine 2001: 15). What this means in practice is that these buildings are seen as playing no role in the heritage of Luang Prabang and can be removed from the landscape. If they are replaced, new buildings should conform to the architectural prescriptions contained in the PSMV. Article 11 of the PSMV states that "any new building will be constructed by respecting the characteristics of one of those architectural models listed in the Fascic[u] le n° 1: Architectural types, of the Recommendation Notebook" (La Maison du Patrimoine 2001: 26). This article then goes on for five pages, describing in detail the construction prescriptions for such buildings.

Fascicule, or Manual, No. 1, entitled *Types Architecturaux* (Architectural Types), is a detailed thirty-three-page document that provides plans, sections, and elevations of each building typology deemed important within the PSMV. Together with Fascicules Nos. 2, 3, and 4, entitled, respectively, Details, Materials, and Colors, Fascicule No. 1 defines with great precision the methods for reconstruction of existing buildings within the PSMV Zone of Preservation. The restoration of torchis, the wattle-and-daub-like construction of woven bamboo and plaster shown in Figure 4.17, and the reconstruction of the

FIGURE 4.17   Torchis construction in historic building (photo by authors).

timber frames that provide the structure for many of these buildings, shown in Figure 4.18, are detailed within the Fascicules.

These prescriptions also govern at least the character of new buildings constructed within the Zone of Preservation, even while the historic methods

FIGURE 4.18   Timber frame under reconstruction, main road Luang Prabang (photo by authors).

are replaced by modern materials. As the next chapter indicates, this process has had several seemingly unintended consequences within the ZPP-Ua, as "white-coded" buildings are replaced with reproductions of historical buildings based on the typologies given in the PSMV Fascicules.

The third and final subcategory of buildings not included in the PSMV inventory are the yellow-coded buildings, light gray in Figure 4.16. These are "buildings perturbing the landscape" (La Maison du Patrimoine 2001: 15)—mostly modern additions to historic buildings. And although they are often integral to the functioning of the existing building, sometimes containing a kitchen or a toilet, or in some instances important retail square footage, they nevertheless are slated for removal.

These classifications and the UNESCO prescriptions that guide the rehabilitation, reconstruction, or demolition of buildings are the keys both to the development of a commodified tourist landscape within the Preservation Zone (ZPP-Ua) and to the emendments that occur within the built environment.

MAKING HERITAGE MANIFEST

It is interesting to analyze the PSMV, its maps and categories and typologies, in the context of the history of Laos and the struggle to define both its physical boundaries and the sociocultural aspects of Lao-ness. In *Creating Laos*, Soren Ivarsson describes the French colonial encounter in Laos as "a French colonial discourse aimed at consolidating and more clearly defining Lao/Laos as a classificatory category. The Lao were made manifest. They could be identified, classified, counted, measured, and compared with other groups of people" (Ivarsson 2008: 25). Thus PSMV's maps similarly attempt to bound Luang Prabang, making its World Heritage status manifest. These maps not only delineate heritage from "not heritage" but also carefully categorize the relative importance of particular pieces of architectural heritage. These maps and their supporting documents allow the counting, measuring, and comparing of all elements of the built environment. They also set in place the foundation for the process of emendment (additions and erasures) that we explore more fully in the next chapter.

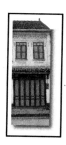

CHAPTER FIVE

EMENDING THE BUILT ENVIRONMENT: ERASURE AND ADDITION IN LUANG PRABANG

Enlarged or diminished, embellished or purified, lengthened or abbreviated, the past becomes more and more a foreign country, yet also increasingly tinged with the present colours. —David Lowenthal (1986)

In Chapter One we discussed the idea of erasure as antithetical to history but simultaneously central to the definition of heritage and of heritage tourism. In this chapter we again approach the idea of erasure, this time with the goal of illuminating instances when erasures have simultaneously assisted in defining the necessary bracketed tourist space and removed physical as well as social space from the landscape of Luang Prabang since its world heritage designation.

Chapter Two laid out a framework that explained various methods and motivations for emendment under conditions of heritage production and provided examples of the processes and products of erasures and additions at various heritage sites around the world. In this chapter we use this framework as our lens of analysis, focusing it on Luang Prabang to show how erasure and addition are enacted in the World Heritage preservation zone and more specifically to show how the built environment plays a central role in these processes. Moving between locations of emendment within the UNESCO zone of preservation, the chapter shows how erasure and addition, understood as synergetic processes, construct meanings for tourists in Luang Prabang while simultaneously serving to solidify the Lao past in service of a unified Lao history.

As we showed in Chapter Three, this Lao past is highly variable and in many respects contested. Through the process of packaging the city's World Heritage, this variable and contested history is simplified, bracketed, and sold to tourists for their consumption. In the process, it serves the needs of the Lao government by capitalizing on the city's built heritage both to attract tourist dollars and to solidify the history of the state. In this project the state walks a fine line between acknowledging the problematic aspects of its own history and the very need to construct Laos as a bounded nation-state whose existence is, as noted in Chapter Three, largely founded on the imaginary of a geographic and sociocultural territory. All the while the ability to market the built environment as well as its meanings to tourists must be maintained. However, as Lowenthal points out, "to specify such motives,... is not to say that all these alterations are deliberate. We are often innocent of conscious intent to change what we mean simply to conserve or celebrate" (Lowenthal 1986: 325).

Chapter Four provided a description of Luang Prabang's architecture and its official classifications within the PSMV preservation documents. The two main classifications of Buildings Inventoried in the PSMV and Buildings Not Inventoried in the PSMV are further subcategorized based on their relative contributions to the World Heritage designation and the degree to which each can be altered under the PSMV regulations. All the buildings within the zone of preservation are placed into these classifications and subcategories.

This chapter is organized as a kind of tourist's walking tour, beginning at the north end of the zone of preservation near the confluence of the Mekong and Nam Khan Rivers. Moving southward, we engage the theme of the erasure—the removal of the physically incongruent, the unpalatable, and the politically inexpedient—as they occur along our path. Along the way we will encounter all the processes of erasure enumerated in Chapter Two, including physical erasure, as well as important additions that follow these erasures and that together help create new meanings in the built environment. Our path, shown in Figure 5.1, will take us from Ban Xieng Thong in the north to Ban Vatthat in the south and then east to the eastern edge of the preservation zone in Ban Meunna.

THE NORTH PENINSULA

We begin our tour at the northern tip of the peninsula where the Nam Khan and Mekong meet. Here a number of guest houses have been recently completed or are in the late stages of reconstruction. Two villages, Ban Xieng Thong and Ban Khili occupy this northern most extreme of the Luang Prabang peninsula. This is the mythical founding place of the city, where two holy men are said to have laid one of the four markers that delimited the city near a tree at the confluence of the Mekong and Nam Khan. The small village of Ban Xieng Thong, anchored by Wat Xieng Thong, the historical royal wat and burial place of King Sisavang Vong, is now known for its paper-making craft. Just north of the stairs that link the wat complex to the Mekong we encounter the first of our erasures, and additions, The Mekong View Hotel, shown in Figure 5.2. This large new hotel complex now looks out over the Mekong, as the name suggests, having replaced several buildings that once stood on the site, as shown in the comparative maps in Figure 5.3.

The Mekong View, run by a Swedish expatriate, is constructed in accordance with the PSMV documents. The billboard advertising its construction, still in place at the time of our fieldwork, portrays the new hotel with drawings that are strikingly similar to the PSMV regulations. As in most architectural drawings, there are no people, no vehicles, no life at all, with the exception of

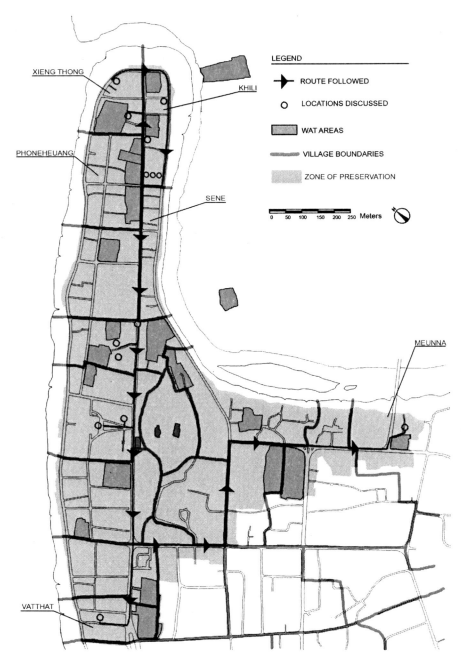

FIGURE 5.1   Walking through Luang Prabang: Sites of Erasure (drawn by authors).

FIGURE 5.2   Mekong View Hotel (photo by authors).

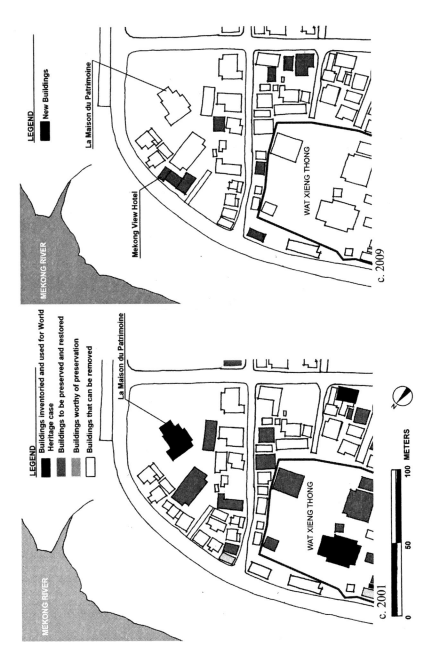

FIGURE 5.3   Enlarged partial maps of Ban Xieng Thong; left, c. 2001, right, c. 2009 (drawn by authors).

the trees. Having removed the physical fabric of the existing village, the hotel now constructs an idealized, albeit oversized, version of what its website calls the "private living quarters in an upscale Lao home" (Paulsson 2008). Aside from its workers, however, there is little about the hotel that is connected to the life of the surrounding village or the nearby Wat Xieng Thong, shown in Figure 5.3. Constructions of this type erase the physically incongruent by replacing the several "white-coded" buildings, shown in the circa 2001 map on the left in Figure 5.3, with structures that match the PSMV exemplars. The New Mekong View Hotel also removes memory and meaning of the place for local residents who may associate the locale with the close-by Wat Xieng Thong and the ceremonial aspects of its connection to the water.

As we move clockwise around the peninsula along the Nam Khan River, we catch glimpses of La Maison du Patrimoine (noted on the map in Figure 5.3 and pictured in Figure 4.13), the structure having been restored to its former glory as the headquarters of the local preservation officials who oversee the Luang Prabang preservation effort. As we turn south along the Nam Khan, we enter Ban Khili, and another new guesthouse comes into view on our right. This guesthouse, shown in Figure 5.4, is much smaller than The Mekong View; its scale is much more in keeping with the surrounding village.

This guesthouse exemplifies the extensive renovation or reconstruction of buildings as guesthouses. This structure was in fact completely rebuilt with modern materials and methods. The building has undergone extensive changes during the reconstruction process including a change in the roof pitch, a change in roof material to meet UNESCO requirements, and the replacement of the traditional building material of torchis. In addition, the building is no longer a village residence but instead now houses eight guest rooms for tourists.

A comparison of the guesthouse in Figure 5.4 and its preconstruction condition, shown in Figure 5.5, exemplifies how reconstructed buildings often bear only a passing resemblance to the original structures that occupied their sites. In conversations with guesthouse proprietors, the disconnection between the goals of the PSMV and the realities of contemporary construction were apparent. Proprietors noted that the PSMV regulations dictated the use of particular forms and materials in reconstruction. Tile, for example, is

FIGURE 5.4   Guesthouse Ban Khili, after reconstruction (photo by authors).

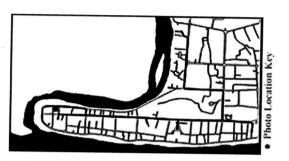

FIGURE 5.5   Guesthouse Ban Khili, before reconstruction, Building 96 of the PSMV Inventory (source: PSMV).

not a roofing material used in all buildings, and in fact many buildings use corrugated metal roofs like that shown in Figure 5.5. Corrugated metal roofs are common as evidenced by a number of still extant examples. The PSMV requirement for tile roofs is based in part on their climatic appropriateness. More important, it also supports their local manufacture and the intangible heritage of the craft of producing the tiles. However, the demand for tiles has outpaced local production capability and has led to their sourcing from Thailand, undermining support for local manufacturing. In addition, several owners that we spoke with wanted to reconstruct their buildings using traditional materials and methods of torchis but were unable to do so, because local contractors were unwilling or unable to build using these methods.

Inventoried as Building 96 in UNESCO documents, the building in Figure 5.5, although not physically incongruent—indeed, it is categorized as a "building to be preserved and restored" in the UNESCO PSMV—has nevertheless been the target of physical emendment, while meeting the letter of the UNESCO regulations for preservation and restoration. The question, given the stark contrast between the buildings in Figures 5.4 and 5.5, is the preservation and restoration of what? And what remains from the building in Figure 5.5?

From this guesthouse, moving southward a short distance along the Nam Khan River on Kingkitsalat Road, we encounter the first instance of disconnect between the UNESCO World Heritage designation and its focus on the tangible and the intangible heritage of Ban Khili. The making of rice cakes is an important part of Ban Khili life. Each morning rice cakes are made in the building shown in Figure 5.6 as well as in several other buildings along this stretch of road. This manufacturing process has traditionally been associated with Ban Khili, where the rice cakes are laid out to dry in the sun on bamboo screens along the Nam Khan River. Although this manufacturing activity is an important part of village life, it is housed in a building designated as replaceable, or "white-coded." Through such labeling, the activity and its social significance have in essence been erased, its importance to the village having been completely ignored by UNESCO documents in favor of buildings of note. Such treatment of this, and other buildings where rice crackers are made in Ban Khili, suggests the potential for the erasures of social structure,

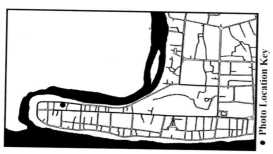

FIGURE 5.6 Making rice crackers, Ban Khili (photo by authors).

memory, and meaning for the residents. This process is indicative of a larger devaluing not only of this particular structure but also of the entire structure of the village and of the everyday activities that take place there. It suggests a failure to recognize the intertwined nature of the physical and the cultural as represented by embedded activities. There is nothing in the PSMV that prevents this site from being converted into a guesthouse or hotel. Nor is there any support for the residents whose manufactory is an important part of Ban Khili life.

A little farther down Kingkitsalat Road we encounter a complex of buildings where physical erasure has again followed from the PSMV "white building" designation of "Buildings which can be replaced." The nearly complete Chang Inn, shown in Figure 5.7, is one of the largest and most elaborate of the guesthouses that have replaced "white-coded" buildings in many locations in Luang Prabang. The complex stretches across almost 40 meters of street frontage, having replaced three buildings, as the comparative maps in Figure 5.8 show. While we cannot know what the original "white-coded" buildings looked like or what role they played in the life of the village, we can, with some certainty conclude that The Chang Inn is remarkably different from the buildings that stood there before its construction.

Although The Chang Inn fulfills the requirements of the PSMV in its use of historically accurate models and massing, the grouping of at least two different exemplars while maintaining uniform color, finish, and detail undoubtedly changes the character of the street. Along other stretches of village streets, this complex of building masses would have formed perhaps four different houses, each with individualized color, finish, and detail. Other blocks also exhibit changes in scale and massing that are absent from The Chang Inn complex. To us, with UNESCO documents in hand, The Chang Inn was an obvious imitation, but we observed tourists photographing this and similar buildings as they toured the city, consuming the "historic" buildings. Finally, like The Mekong View, The Chang Inn erases all village life, like that seen in Figure 5.6.

Turning west just past The Chang Inn, we pass two more new guesthouses as we move up the hill toward Sakkaline Road. Once out on Sakkaline Road, the main north-south route through town, we encounter several historic buildings

Photo Location Key

FIGURE 5.7 The Chang Inn (photo by authors).

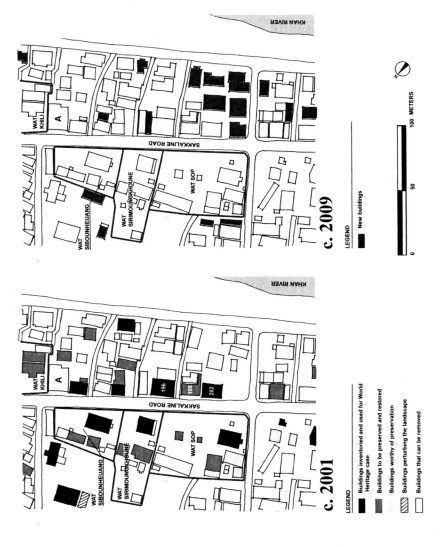

FIGURE 5.8   Enlarged partial maps of Ban Khili; left, c. 2001, right, c. 2009 (drawn by authors).

noted in the UNESCO documents. These include buildings 282 (Figure 5.9), 105, and 196 and across the street to the west, Wat Sop (all identified in c. 2001 map, Figure 5.8).

Immediately behind building 282 once stood a building noted in the PSMV as worthy of preservation and restoration. This building has now been removed and is being replaced with the building shown in Figure 5.10. The building is constructed, like most new structures in the city, of concrete and brick infill. The exterior of the building will likely meet the letter of the PSMV requirements that "any new building will be constructed by respecting the characteristics of one of those architectural models listed in the Fascicule N°1," which delineate approved architectural types. However, it is far from meeting the UNESCO heritage preservation goal of reproducing original construction types and is an example of the introduction of modern materials noted in *Impact* (UNESCO 2004: 47). Its reconstruction also does little to pass on the intangible heritage connected with such local building techniques as torchis, which is also climatically more appropriate. The aforementioned new building and others like it now all but surround buildings 282, 105, and 196, as the enlarged plan of the area in Figure 5.8 shows.

Continuing north on Sakkaline Road we encounter another piece of Luang Prabang's history that has been authorized for removal in the PSMV. On our right just before Wat Khili is the building noted as A on the enlarged maps in Figure 5.8 and shown in Figure 5.11. This concrete building from the mid-twentieth century is a handsome example of the modernist idiom in the colonial context. Its stark white façade, flat concrete eyebrow awnings, and vividly colored shutters set it off along the main road. Buildings of this style are prevalent in the Zone of Preservation and represent a history that is completely devalued in the PSMV. All these buildings are noted in the PSMV as "Buildings that can be removed." If removed, they will necessarily be replaced with buildings like The Chang Inn, The Mekong View, and other reasonable facsimiles of historic structures, as the PSMV dictates.

In contrast to the devaluing of the "white-coded buildings," "black-coded buildings" are many times lavishly restored for tourist uses. Aside from these lavish restorations, such as that of building 282 shown in

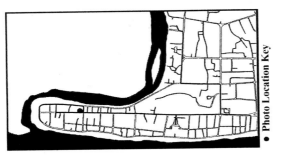

FIGURE 5.9   Building 282 of the PSMV Inventory (photo by authors).

FIGURE 5.10 New building under construction, Ban Khili (photo by authors).

FIGURE 5.11 Building A (see plan Figure 5.8); "white-coded building" just south of Wat Khili (photo by authors).

Figure 5.9, an alternative fate of neglect seems to await other "black-coded" buildings in the PSMV Inventory. These are exemplified in the small residential building shown in Figure 5.12, inventoried as Building 100 in the PSMV. Just off Sakkaline Road in Ban Xieng Thong, this building shows how smaller residential structures, this one near the rear entry of Wat Xieng Thong, have been left to deteriorate. This deterioration is likely due to one of two causes.

The first possibility is that the cost of the restoration required by the PSMV prescriptions is beyond the means of the owner. The second is that the size and the restricted space around the building for expansion limit its economic potential as a tourist venture. In either case, the comparison in Figure 5.12 of the PSMV Inventory photo from 2001 of the building and the building's state of repair in 2008 shows that the building has had little if any work done to preserve it, even though it is "exemplary." This situation is in marked contrast to that of the large sums of money spent to recreate marketable guesthouse facsimiles, such as The Mekong View and The Chang Inn. The second fate of "black-coded buildings," similar to those used for tourists, is illustrated by PSMV-inventoried Building 195, shown in Figure 5.13. This residential building, very close to Building 100, has been extensively restored as a private residence. Given the average income in Laos, this restoration seems extraordinary and suggests either foreign capital or ownership by a member of the very small Laotian elite. Colin Long notes that "for some Lao—especially members of the burgeoning urban middle class —traditional housing is becoming consciously traditional: that is, its meaning has become for these people primarily aesthetic or bound up in a heritage consciousness" (Long 2003: 185).

Reflecting on the process and products of erasure, as we backtrack south along Sakkaline Road to leave Ban Khili and Ban Xieng Thong, we have little doubt that these two villages are rapidly becoming a tourist space rather than a living landscape. This transformation results from the nearly complete severing of the integral link between the built environment as a framework for social structure and the meaning, memory, and daily life of village residents. The linkages between the built environment and the

FIGURE 5.12　Building 100 of the PSMV Inventory; left, Inventory photo, c. 2001; right, c. 2008 (photos by authors).

Figure 5.13   Building 195 of the PSMV Inventory, residence Ban Phoneheuang (photo by authors).

daily rhythms of rice cracker production and a connection to the village wat are quickly giving way to a tourist landscape of guesthouses, where the erasure of the physically incongruent leads to erosion of the social meanings and structure that have for centuries defined the landscape of these two villages.

THE MAIN ROAD

As we approach the center of town on Sakkaline Road there is a shift in the scale of buildings from the village residential to the commercial buildings that line the road. At the same time there is an increase in visibly tourist-oriented spaces and in the number of tourists. Buildings on this stretch of Sakkaline Road, shown in Figures 5.14a and b, especially those of significance, have been almost entirely given over to tourist uses. Internet cafés, restaurants, and hotels occupy nearly all the buildings noted in the PSMV for preservation including "red-coded" and "black-coded" buildings. These tourist-oriented buildings are many times lavished with expensive restorations, which are indeed preserving the physical but not the social space of Luang Prabang. Figure 5.14a shows historic shop houses along Sakkaline Road, where every ground floor space is given over to shops and restaurants catering to tourists. The upper floors of some of these buildings contain guesthouses. The opposite side of the street is similarly given over to uses catering to tourists. Figure 5.14b shows how erasure of "white-coded buildings" along this commercial street results in the addition of replicas of shop houses matching the PSMV requirements but not able to recreate the subtle interplay of materiality, rhythm, massing, and scale. This results in inelegant and ungainly buildings such as that shown at the right in Figure 5.14b.

INNER BLOCKS: REMNANTS OF THE EVERYDAY

The construction of the tourist landscape described above along the main roads is also transforming the life of the inner blocks in the city. These inner blocks have been quite literally surrounded by the tourist landscape, as the

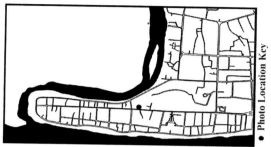

FIGURE 5.14 (A) Sakkaline Road (photo by authors).

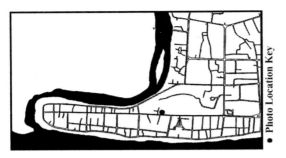

FIGURE 5.14   (B) Sakkaline Road (photo by authors).

enlarged maps in Figure 5.15 show. This tourist landscape is beginning to push toward the middle of the blocks with the extension of tourist uses in new and renovated buildings (Figure 5.15). The peripheral buildings of the block facing the main roads become the tourists' domain, simultaneously cutting the inner blocks off from neighboring blocks. These inner blocks represent some of the last remnants of village life on the peninsula. The still 'living' inner block in Figure 5.16 shows the inseparable relationship between the village sociocultural landscape and the built environment.

In contrast, The Heuanchan (Moon House) Complex run by La Maison du Patrimoine, shown in Figure 5.17, highlights the effect of heritage erasures that separate the sociocultural structure of the village from the built environment, devaluing the former while valorizing the latter. The Heuanchan structure, an inner block building that was once part of the local village, has been reconstructed by La Maison du Patrimoine as a visitors' center to showcase the architecture of the village. Yet the reconstruction has removed all parts of the village other than the physical structure, in the process sanitizing the place, removing scooters, laundry, residents, food preparation, animals, and people, all of which tourists may in some way find unpalatable. Having separated the two and having turned the built into something that can be sold to tourists for their consumption, the synergistic combination of the social and physical, that which heritage tourists indeed are seeking and which the UNESCO World Heritage designation sought to preserve, has all but disappeared.

THE NATIONAL MUSEUM

As we re-enter the main street and turn south, approaching the former Royal Palace complex, now the National Museum, the road's name changes from Sakkaline Road to Sisavang Vong Road. On our right stands the new temple built to house the Pra Bang Buddha. Just beyond we encounter the gates of the National Museum with its *allée* of palm trees leading to the main building. On the opposite side of the street rises Mount Phousi, topped with the That Chomsi Stupa. The change of the street name to that of the last officially

FIGURE 5.15   Enlarged partial map of central Luang Prabang; left, c. 2001; right, c. 2009 (drawn by authors).

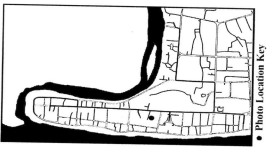

FIGURE 5.16   Inner block, Building 228 of the PSMV Inventory (photo by authors).

FIGURE 5.17 Heuanchan complex, Building 119 of the PSMV Inventory (photo by authors).

crowned King of Laos is a concrete manifestation of the former royal family and its importance in the national history. Employing the name of the King highlights the tension between the Lao past and the Lao present. The Lao past is grounded in the relationship between Theravada Buddhism, the royal lineage, and the Pra Bang statue. As noted in Chapter Three, the Pra Bang served as a palladium for the monarchy, safeguarding the kingdom of Lan Xang and later Luang Prabang. Together these elements defined the political culture and legitimized the rule of the royal family. In the Lao present, without king or royal lineage, the Marxist State has sought legitimation through the invocation of a Lao past, albeit one where certain elements have been obscured. At the National Museum, pictured in Figure 5.18, the tension between past and present is only thinly veiled. In the museum, the former king's personal effects and living quarters are on display, but at the same time there is no mention of the last heir to the throne.[1] His removal from the throne to a "seminar camp" and his eventual death there are erased from present memory and heritage displays. This piece of history is "forgotten" —that is, omitted—as it might prove difficult for the current government to explain Savang Vatthana's fate to locals and tourists alike and might prove inconvenient in their effort to construct a unified Lao nation.

The selling of Luang Prabang to tourists and its preservation as a UNESCO World Heritage Site, defined in part by French Colonial rule and the architecture that accompanied it, requires the connection to the Lao royal past, while at the same time the LPDR relies on an imagined Lao past to legitimize itself and the unified Lao nation-state. Although these two aims are, as Long and Sweet (2006) have argued, largely compatible, the present LPDR government attempts to erase from memory particular pieces of Luang Prabang's history that would have the potential to undermine its legitimacy. Although Long and Sweet's argument is a compelling one, and when considered in the abstract is simple enough, the situation is considerably complicated by the

---

[1]Crown Prince Savang Vatthana was named Regent when his father Sisavang Vong became ill. Upon his father's death on October 29, 1959, he informally ascended the throne. He was never officially crowned king, deferring his coronation until the cessation of civil war.

FIGURE 5.18   Former Royal Palace, now The National Museum, Building 389 of the PSMV Inventory (photo courtesy of Sebastian Friedrich).

existence of the former Royal Palace. This building is a key component of defining the colonial heritage of Luang Prabang because of the intertwined nature of the colonial administration and the King, as the history in Chapter Three illustrates. Thus, although the King himself can and has been physically erased, his former residence, an important piece of colonial architecture, cannot realistically be removed, because it is a key element of the World Heritage designation.

Despite the contradiction between Buddhist and Marxist worldviews, and the fact that the LPDR may find the Prabang Buddha inconvenient because of its historical relationship to the royal house and Buddhism, it cannot easily be erased. Residing now in the new temple on the grounds of the National Museum (Figure 5.19), the Pra Bang is the central player in yearly ceremonies even as these ceremonies become presentations for tourists rather than ritualistic performance and practice by residents. Similar transformations are also evident in *binthabat*, the early morning ritual of alms giving, that takes place throughout the city (Dioko and Gujadhur 2008). The giving of alms each morning embodies the reciprocal relationship that links residents to monks from their local wat.

This relationship and the meaning embodied by the daily ceremonial act are in danger of being erased in the tourist landscape. Each morning, busloads of tourists line the streets awaiting the monks and the opportunity to photograph this important cultural practice. The process has become a spectacle for tourists who often fail to understand the significance of the daily event in the lives of the residents or the culturally specific rules of the practice (UNESCO 2004). As Dioko and Gujadhur note, portions of the alms route are now "packaged" for tourists, "and local residents position themselves in other less obtrusive routes" (Dioko and Gujadhur 2008: 3). This shift in the relationship of residents with their built environment, as well as the relocation of local residents from the city's core to more peripheral residential areas through the process of developing a tourist landscape, alters and weakens the relationship between residents and their village wat. The wat is left as a physical remnant, but the underlying cultural network of reciprocal support is undermined.

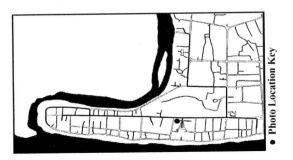

FIGURE 5.19   New temple on the grounds of The National Museum (photo by authors).

These transformations highlight the central position of cultural activities related to Theravada Buddhism in the life of Luang Prabang, and how World Heritage status and the resultant tourism alter those activities and their meanings. Furthermore, because these cultural activities are inseparable from the built environment, the transformation of the physical landscape has commensurate effects on the city's cultural heritage, both tangible and intangible. Finally, they are also indicative of the dilemma that World Heritage tourism presents in places that excite tourists through their extraordinary qualities but that at the same time have fragile and contested cultural heritages. Like the packaging of any commodity for consumption, the packaging of heritage, tangible or intangible, has the potential to alter, one may even argue necessarily alters, the very heritages that are seen as valuable. While the packaging is not "bad" in and of itself, and indeed culture is fluid and continuously changing, when those most affected by the packaging are left out of the process of deciding how and what will be packaged, then the process must be questioned.

Thus La Maison du Patrimoine, as the local authority in charge of overseeing the implementation of the PSMV, must walk the fine line between acknowledging a Lao past in which Theravada Buddhism and the Royal family were the key elements of a complex multi-ethnic Lao social structure and working within the Lao political paradigm that seeks to define a unified Marxist state in the Lao present. The difficulty here is well stated by Stuart-Fox: "The leaders of the Lao People's Revolutionary Party (LPRP) have sought to undermine the traditional legitimacy which Buddhism accorded the former regime, and to establish new ideological justification for their own exercise of political authority" (Stuart-Fox 1983: 428). This attempt to undermine Theravada Buddhism took place, as Stuart-Fox points out, in the context of an already weakened role for both the Lao Royal family and Buddhism brought on by French Colonial rule and by the postcolonial Royal Lao Government. Although more recently, in the wake of economic liberalization in the 1990s, the government has softened its stance vis-à-vis Buddhism and the Sangha, the inherent tension still exists between Buddhist and Marxist worldviews that "could hardly be more different" (Stuart-Fox 1983: 440).

GUESTHOUSE LANDSCAPES

The increasing numbers of tourist arrivals in Luang Prabang have not only led to the repackaging of the Lao past; it has also fueled a commensurate increase in the number of hotels to house the tourists. Hotel accommodation in the city rose 49 percent between 2001 and 2006 (Travers 2007: 112). We have already seen a number of new accommodations at the north end of the Luang Prabang peninsula. Leaving the National Museum complex and moving south, we encounter a large number of new guesthouses.

During our survey of the zone of preservation it became apparent that these new guesthouses are replacing large parts of the existing building stock and the life that once accompanied it. In particular, at the south end of the Preservation Zone, in Ban Vatthat and Ban Houaxieng, guesthouses have all but replaced the life of entire stretches of the inner lanes running from the Mekong to the Main Road. The inner blocks in this area are now filled with less expensive accommodations targeted at young backpackers. While this transformation erases the areas' social fabric, it also erases the physical land-scape that is inappropriate for tourist housing. The landscape is replaced with guesthouses like the one in Figure 5.20, which depicts at the left the house as inventoried in the PSMV in 2001 and at the right the new structure that had replaced it by 2008.

PSMV-inventoried Building 237 is another example of the fate that awaits the "black-coded" buildings of the PSMV (those that constituted the justifica-tion for UNESCO World Heritage status) and that show the process of erasure. The example in Figure 5.21 shows how the process of erasure can work in some cases. On the left, is the building as it existed in 2001; on the right, its condition in 2008.

The building has been completely removed, its timbers now piled at the center of the site presumably awaiting reconstruction. As of the summer of 2009, the building remained unreconstructed. The comparative maps in Figure 5.22 illustrate how these emendments are enacted in this considerably more dense urban environment. The result is an increasingly dense fabric of less expensive tourist accommodations and the erasure of the existing village milieu.

FIGURE 5.20   Guesthouse in Ban Vatthat, Building 238 of the PSMV Inventory; left, Inventory photo, c. 2001, right, c. 2008 (photos by authors).

FIGURE 5.21   Ban Vatthat, Building 237 of the PSMV Inventory; left, Inventory photo, c. 2001, right, c. 2008 (photos by authors).

FIGURE 5.22   Enlarged partial map, Ban Vatthat; left, c. 2001, right, c. 2009 (drawn by authors).

RECREATING AN IMAGINED COLONIAL PAST

To conclude our walking tour we jump now from this guesthouse landscape, moving quickly through town past several markets to the eastern reaches of the zone of preservation. Moving east down Vatmou-Enna Road toward the boundary of the Zone of Preservation, we encounter far fewer tourists. Near the eastern extreme of the Zone of Preservation, we wander into the grounds of what at first looks like a garden. It turns out to be The Villa Maydou (Figure 5.23), a boutique hotel housed in two historic buildings inventoried in the PSMV.

Although we are very near to the traffic of the main bridge across the Nam Khan River, the noise of traffic is almost non-existent. We have jumped not only from the heavily tourist-oriented landscape of central Luang Prabang but also seemingly in time, The Villa Maydou recreating a romanticized vision of colonial life. This landscape has been cleansed of all modern detritus. This is perhaps the penultimate space of erasure, a place where tourists, at least those who can afford it, can immerse themselves in an imagined colonial space, where the real world of twenty-first-century Laos cannot intrude.

ROUTES THROUGH THE PAST

David Lowenthal, in his seminal work *The Past Is a Foreign Country*, suggests that "memory, history, and relics offer routes to the past best traversed in combination" (Lowenthal 1986: 249). Our path through the UNESCO Zone of Preservation in Luang Prabang highlights the interconnection of these three factors while bringing to the fore the importance of the relic as it manifests itself as the built environment. The relics of Luang Prabang, as they are emended, offer multiple routes through the city's past and present. These routes support multiple visions: UNESCO's for the World Heritage City, the Lao government's for their construction of a Lao Nation-State, and tourists' for an extraordinary and exotic experience. These visions are at times convergent and at times divergent, but they intersect in the built environment of Luang Prabang. The process of emendment described here preserves the physical

FIGURE 5.23   Villa Maydou, Building 266 of the PSMV Inventory (photo by authors).

relics that define Luang Prabang as an outpost of French colonial expansion for UNESCO; for the government it helps to solidify a unified Lao past that the nation requires to unite the Lao people in the present; and for tourists it helps to fulfill a nostalgic desire. *Our* route through Luang Prabang highlights the places where these visions intersect and conflict and provides the opportunity for the visitor, the tourist, and the residents of Luang Prabang's living landscapes to understand alternate histories, their removal from the landscape, and their potential as heritage.

CHAPTER SIX

A DIALOGUE: GLOBAL FLOWS AND LOCAL CULTURE

Tourism is both putting pressure on local communities and their resources, whether economic, environmental or cultural, while simultaneously offering new possibilities to diversify incomes…. Ubiquitously tourism is changed and is changing economic, social and cultural systems.
—John Connell and Barbara Rugendyke (2008)

PERSPECTIVES ON INCONVENIENT HERITAGE

Heritage performed as part of everyday life is evident in the relics that make up the physical environment. This heritage can also be packaged and presented for tourists in more intentional ways. Today certain aspects of heritage may resonate with local residents whose history it represents, whereas other aspects may resonate more with various segments of global tourists.

131

Indeed, some scholars have suggested that presentations of heritage, whether "fake" or "genuine," are driven by judgments about the market for such heritage. Harrison offers a particularly insightful assertion in that regard:

> Most of all, what is defined as heritage is linked to *power*: The power to impose a view of the world, especially of the past, on others. Perceptions of the past are closely linked to present hierarchies, and the voices of those at the top are often the most likely to prevail. By contrast, the voices of the most lowly stakeholders—whose houses were built of wood or thatch rather than stone—are muted or silent... (Harrison 2005a: 7; emphasis in original)

Globalization, although a term often overused and ill defined, aptly circumscribes many of these present hierarchies and power structures. Globalization and global flows exert considerable influence within the socio-spatial realm and are particularly salient in the context of Luang Prabang's emergence as a tourist destination.

GLOBAL FLOWS: STALLMEYER

The Luang Prabang case represents an instance when larger processes of globalization are manifested in the built environment. The processes of UNESCO World Heritage nomination and designation, and the application of subsequent planning documents, are themselves manifestations of a globalized heritage discourse and regime. The tourists that follow such designations embody global flows of people, images, and capital. Together these processes introduce a new set of global influences to the social and physical realms within Luang Prabang that necessarily bring about change at the local scale. This perspective informs my analysis of the changes to the city's built environment. I believe that the capital that comes with World Heritage designation both from tourists and from international aid is perhaps the most powerful of these flows. It has the capability, when combined with a global tourist media, to commodify the urbanism of Luang Prabang.

The representations of heritage consciously displayed in Luang Prabang and the initial process of inscription of Luang Prabang as a UNESCO World Heritage Site are linked to the power of both the UNESCO-affiliated advisors and the national and local governments. The perspective of UNESCO-affiliated advisors, such as Les Atelier de la Péninsule, who prepared the Luang Prabang World Heritage nomination file, provided the initial framework by which the city's heritage was categorized and displayed (Atelier de la Péninsule 2004). In fact, it appears that Les Atelier de la Péninsule, as one of the "interested parties looking out for the city's welfare" (Barnett 1996: 4), was instrumental in suggesting that Luang Prabang, as "the best preserved traditional city in South East Asia" (Barnett 1996: 4), be conserved and saved from modernization resulting from a major highway designed to pass through Luang Prabang's peninsula. The initial framework generated by Les Atelier de la Péninsule was further elaborated and approved as regulation in April 2001 (Ministry of Information and Culture—Lao PDR 2003b). The worldview represented by the national government is imprinted on the fabric of the city through the process of nomination that moves documents upward through the governmental chain of command from the Department of Museums and Archaeology, to the Ministry of Information and Culture, to the National Committee of Preservation of Historical, Cultural and Natural Heritage, and finally to the Prime Minister's Office for endorsement and proclamation (Ministry of Information and Culture—Lao PDR 2003a). The influence of the local government in the display of heritage is ensured through the PSMV regulations that are enforced by the municipal authorities through La Maison du Patrimoine.

The original threat to the colonial urbanism of Luang Prabang, and one that precipitated its UNESCO designation, was the planned construction of a highway linking the Lao Capital of Vientiane to China; it would have cut through Luang Prabang's old town. In part to halt this global process of connection and the flows that would follow, interested parties such as the architects François Greck and Jean-Christophe Marchal of Les Atelier de la Péninsule promoted the importance of preserving Luang Prabang through World Heritage Site designation (Barnett 1996). Nevertheless, the city has been transformed; differently (presumably better) to be sure, but changed irrevocably. And this irrevocable change has erased much of the underlying social and cultural landscape. This landscape was the palimpsest on which Luang Prabang's thousand-year history was written again and again.

LOCAL CULTURE: DEARBORN

As Harrison (2005) rightly points out, the voices of the lowly stakeholders, the village residents in the case of Luang Prabang, are muted by adherence to the aforementioned top-down structure. International scholars have critiqued the limited community voices in the initial process and in the current process of tourism development in the city. Working in concert with UNESCO to suggest a process for tourism management in Luang Prabang, these scholars have repeatedly suggested that "the people of Luang Prabang need to determine if the current style of tourism development... is appropriate in terms of their long-term goals" (UNESCO 2004: 77). Furthermore, they highlight the lack of resident participation in a local comprehensive planning process as having reduced the benefit of heritage tourism for the community as a whole. This reduced benefit to the community leads us to question the purpose for and processes of heritage development in Luang Prabang both as a node in global flows of international tourists and as a living landscape facilitating and/ or inhibiting the everyday life of residents.

One of the primary reasons that tourists visit Luang Prabang is to experience the town's religious heritage, which is grounded in a unique form of Theravada Buddhism (SNUV survey noted in UNESCO 2004: 54). Laotian Buddhism is interwoven with animist worship of local protective spirits known as *phi* as well as remnants of Brahmanic rituals such as worship of the *naga*, a deity that takes the form of a hooded snake. The primacy of Theravada Buddhism in Luang Prabang is physically evident in the twenty village-temple complexes within the PSMV-designated Preservation Zone identified in Figure 4.2, and also in the daily rhythms of Luang Prabang's residents. The village temple complex and the reciprocal relationship between the wat's monks and village residents underpin the norms, beliefs, social activities, and cultural practices of Luang Prabang's residents. One need spend only a short time in Luang Prabang observing and listening to absorb the importance of Theravada Buddhism in the city.

Today, Theravada Buddhism has rebounded to a place of personal importance for most residents of Luang Prabang after nearly twenty years of government restrictions on religious practice, from 1975 to the early 1990s. UNESCO World Heritage designation and the resulting influx of international tourists interested in the city's religious heritage give the city's residents new reasons to take pride in their Buddhist heritage and offer a safe place for religious practice. However, a pivotal question as yet unasked of the city's residents is this: to what degree do they wish to have tourists intrude into their personal and community religious life?

Dioko and Gujadhur (2008) have noted with regard to the performance of particular Buddhist rituals that UNESCO World Heritage designation with its particular set of regulations regarding the preservation of heritage and with the resulting flows of global tourists has affected local sociocultural productions. Likewise, we have highlighted some of the influences of UNESCO World Heritage designation, as a global force, on other everyday activities and on relationships among the city's villages.

Luang Prabang offers tourists an unusual glance at an extraordinary physical and sociocultural environment. In his book *The Tourist Gaze*, John Urry highlights that, as modern-day tourists identify possible destinations around the world, they seek locations where they can gaze on something extraordinary that will take them away from the ordinary experiences of their routine lives (2002). Thus, global tourists who arrive in Luang Prabang are currently rewarded as they walk through the city. In this regard, tourists to Luang Prabang can be compared to those discussed by Phillip Duke in his book *The Tourist Gaze, the Cretans Glance*, who are rewarded by their glance at the constructed and bracketed archeological heritage of the "glorious Minoan monarchy" presented at Knossos (2007: 120). In a similar fashion, the heritage of Luang Prabang has been constructed and bracketed to present global tourists with an extraordinary glance at an ancient urban environment with a romanticized colonial past.

As mentioned, Luang Prabang came to the notice of international tourists through its 1995 listing as a UNESCO World Heritage City. It is the city's physical fabric made of villages and an architecture offering a unique blending of traditional Laotian architectural styles with French colonial and Vietnamese design elements that recommend this place to tourists seeking an extraordinary experience as they escape from their everyday lives. However, the increasing influx of tourists over the last fourteen years and transformations in the built environment designed to respond to the needs and desires of international tourists threaten to undermine the very tangible and intangible qualities that tourists seek when they visit the city.

The question therefore is how to invest local stakeholders with a meaningful role in maintaining Luang Prabang's tangible and intangible qualities for the future. In the dialogue that follows we explore our understanding of how, in the broadest terms, this may be possible.

AUTHORS' DIALOGUE

Stallmeyer: So what if they had decided to have a more participatory process—how would that have made things different?

Dearborn: It could have "museumized" the place in the same way that we saw in Hoi An. There would be certain places that you could go and other places where residents would have the power to say "We don't want you to go there." You could have a series of tickets for certain places and others would be private. That's one way that residents could have a say in preserving their private lives. So tourists wouldn't feel comfortable going around essentially peeking in people's kitchen windows.

Stallmeyer: But that still changes the culture and social life of the place—it's just changing in a different way.

Dearborn: Exactly, but it's changing in a way that local people have more control over. The question is, who gets to decide that enough is enough in any particular situation?

Stallmeyer: From my perspective that is an interesting question: "who decides" is an interesting question. Because right now it seems to me that the global market, embodied in tourist flows and expectations, is deciding. But the other interesting question is as soon as you conceive of yourself as presenting something to someone else or that you see something as having value outside of its social or cultural value for you or for your community that immediately changes the way that you see it. As soon as you plan for it you've altered it.

Dearborn: But if you don't plan for it you also alter it. So my point is, shouldn't the people who have to inhabit that environment on a daily basis be the ones who are deciding. And I understand that they may not be the most informed decision makers on certain levels, but maybe if the consequences of certain decisions were laid out, the local residents could be more informed.

Stallmeyer: But, on the other hand, they may already be much more informed about what makes the community continue to be viable as a community. So what happens if they want to tear down certain buildings?

Dearborn: Well, that is the other side of it.

Stallmeyer: What if they don't see the heritage that UNESCO sees as of Outstanding Universal Value, as valuable?

Dearborn: If that is the case, then they have to understand the balance—that is, you lose your World Heritage designation, which may or may not affect the tourist dollars coming in. I mean I assume that revenue would eventually go down.

Stallmeyer: Maybe, but maybe not. Because it's already changing, what is going on now is going to influence who comes there to see what. And the question is, and this is the central point for me, as soon as you put yourself onto this global stage and say come here and see this, then you've opened yourself up for change.

Dearborn: Yes, but at what point do you get fed up with people peeking in your kitchen windows? And shouldn't the resident have some say in the degree of what happens? What the regulation says, the point at which the regulation influences their lives?

Stallmeyer: So you are suggesting a way for them to control the flows of globalization at least to a degree?

Dearborn: Yes, in a certain way, to act in a local sense. And it might be that certain people would decide that they don't want to go to Luang Prabang, because they aren't going to get to see what they want to see. But I would doubt that scenario based on cases like Hoi An. Because The Hoi An case shows that saying, for example, "These three temples are temples you can visit; and you can get your ticket to visit those; and these houses are ones that you can visit," can work.

Stallmeyer: It's a little artificial, but no more so than in Luang Prabang right now—maybe even less where the whole peninsula is becoming a sort of Main Street Disneyland of "Lao-French" reproductions.

Dearborn: And right now you don't pay to see anything in Luang Prabang. You do pay to see Wat Xieng Thong, but not any of the other wats, and there is no revenue stream coming back to the entire community. Individual households that have some sort of entrepreneurial activity may have a personal revenue stream. But the point is that if there were some sort of regulation there would be a little bit more control over invasion of tourists into everyday life, and there would potentially be a more consistent revenue stream that benefited the entire population.

And so in that way it feeds back to the global stream, but it gives the local population a way to determine their own destiny in a certain sense and provide for general maintenance and some of the other things that could sustain the community, where that money is coming from international aid right now. So it has the potential to give the local population more power. This controls where the global flow is felt. And right now they only have that on the basis of "I can make my house a guest house or I can set up my shop to sell to tourists."

Stallmeyer: That's important, because right now everyone is forced to deal with the flow of tourists, and we know it has altered the alms-giving in communities. And that's the reason we don't have any photos of the alms-giving, because we were uncomfortable participating in the spectacle. I was thinking about this as I was looking through our photos of the central block areas, where we were essentially wandering around in those people's front yard. We were careful to get their permission as best we could, but I could see that becoming annoying as the number of tourists venturing off the main streets increases.

Dearborn: Yes, and that is a very different experience than the one that has been set up at Heuanchan, which is completely fictive, and there is no life going on there. There weren't people washing clothes or fixing their motorcycles. So what I want to know as a global tourist is, how does daily life occur?

Stallmeyer: So what we are suggesting is that the situation is dichotomous; on the one hand, you have The Moon House that is completely sanitized in the service of global tourists but no one is too interested in it, as evidenced by the very few people we saw there. And on the other extreme, you have the place where there is no sanitizing but also no flow of global capital to those people, and they are essentially not benefiting directly from the heritage that they are displaying or carrying on, and what you are suggesting is that there is some middle ground where they, instead of us wandering around their yard, would have a mechanism to decide how people would access that space.

Dearborn: Yes, which means that there are certain locations that are packaged. That the local population has said are OK places where tourists can interact with their culture.

Stallmeyer: But that is a very difficult thing.

Dearborn: Right but at least the local community gets to decide that points A, B, and C are places where we let tourists see certain parts of the culture. And, yes, it will change the nature of the display to a more conscious one in those locations.

Stallmeyer: But that has always been the case.

Dearborn: Yes, and my point is the local population needs to make those decisions and benefit from this in a way that they don't benefit from it right now. So members of the local population actually gain in both areas. They gain in the ability to carry out their lives not under surveillance all the time. And they benefit from some kind of revenue stream that is more consistent and more uniform across the population. And that doesn't mean that the entrepreneurs aren't continuing to benefit, but it means that the people who live in the inner block are benefiting, too.

Stallmeyer: That would be a means for the local population to gain a degree of control rather than some higher authority saying "we are going to accept global flows, and so be it."

Dearborn: Right, it has really been a very top-down process. Although there has been some interaction with the village headmen and the heads of some temples, that doesn't necessarily mean that it has penetrated through to the entire population or that the headmen have educated the entire population on the options.

Stallmeyer: Yes, especially since there is a power relationship that is unacknowledged.

Dearborn: So if you compare it to the Fiji example, where The Great Council of Chiefs has ultimate authority over the country's government, and they have members that are distributed throughout the country, and they are powerful on a local level but they are also beholden to their entire village in their national decision-making capacity.

Stallmeyer: Then my question is, what does this do to The UNESCO framework where World Heritage is constructed as bigger than any local community and that somehow I should be able to decide if something is important and if the locals decide that it is not important I can still say it is important.

Dearborn: But you can't say that.

Stallmeyer: But under the UNESCO framework I can?

Dearborn: You can say that it is important as World Heritage, but if the local states' party doesn't accept that, then it goes away. UNESCO may decide that is important, but there is a process for delisting. And now we have cases of delisting, and that is the point where the local population decides that the regulations are intrusive and decides that they are not going to follow them. Once that happens, over a period of time and given enough degradation of the conditions that supported World Heritage status, then the status is removed.

The point is that I don't actually think the locals are really deciding. The tour operators who bring tourists to watch the alms-giving are not local people. They are not representing the local sentiment, but they are profiting from the display and stripping it of its meaning.

Stallmeyer: What I think is interesting is that we come at this and see the Luang Prabang case from very different perspectives. I seem always to be looking at the top-down forces, and you always seem to be looking from the bottom-up. And yet we both are concluding that the central question in these types of case where there are real people in a living landscape is—**who decides?**

Dearborn: Exactly. And at the same time, we both see the cultural realm and the physical as inseparable. The limited acknowledgment of this inseparability in the initial listing process is one of the failures of the UNESCO model as deployed in Luang Prabang.

EPILOGUE

During the research and writing of this book, the transformation of Luang Prabang has continued, but not without notice. Perhaps most important, UNESCO scrutiny of the transformations we have noted throughout this book has increased. In March of 2008, UNESCO published the results of their Reactive Mission to The Town of Luang Prabang, although it was not available publicly until several months later. In this report they call special attention to the "demolition and reconstruction of listed properties" and the "over-densification of urban fabric" (Boccardi and Logan 2007: 2), two phenomena that were clearly evident to us. They call attention to the city's wats and the erosion of the sociospatial relationship between village residents and wats based on alms-giving.

Furthermore, at its 32nd session, the UNESCO World Heritage Committee noted that "the level of coordination and the priority given to protection of the property's Outstanding Universal Value has been insufficient to halt the progressive loss of its fabric and its traditions in the face of development pressures" (World Heritage Committee 2008: 105). From our perspective, it is interesting to note that many of these development pressures are a direct result of the tourism that followed from the city's World Heritage designation. They also note, however, the commitment of the State Party to "strengthen coordination with local stakeholders at the site" (World Heritage Committee 2008: 105). Our hope is that the State Party uses the broadest definition of local stakeholders—although given the pressure for development capital, we are not sanguine in this regard.

Without a broad definition and the integration of local residents into the process—and a meaningful mechanism for local residents to determine the future of their city—degradation of the city under tourist development pressures seems likely to continue. UNESCO is clear about actions to be taken if this situation should indeed continue. They will "[consider] in the absence of substantial progress, the inscription of the property on the List of World Heritage in Danger." This is the first step to either improvement or delisting, the latter having taken place twice, in 2007 for Oman's Arabian Oryx Sanctuary and in June of 2009 for Dresden's Elbe Valley.

We remain hopeful that the lessons learned from the Luang Prabang case and the small contribution this book may have made in establishing the inseparability of the social and physical realms in living landscapes may provide assistance to future locations deemed sites of outstanding universal value.

Lynne M. Dearborn and John C. Stallmeyer

REFERENCES

Ahrentzen, Sherry, and Kathryn H. Anthony. 1993. Sex, stars, and studios: A look at gendered educational practices in architecture. *Journal of Architectural Education* 47(1): 11–29.

AlSayyad, Nezar, Ed. 2001. Consuming tradition, manufacturing heritage: Global norms and urban forms in the age of tourism, p. 3. London: Routledge.

Atelier de la Péninsule. 2004. *Luang Phabang*. Vientiane, Laos: Atelier de la Péninsule Co. Ltd.

Australian ICOMOS Secretariat. 1999. Burra Charter. A. ICOMOS, Ed. Queen Victoria Terrace, ACT: Australian ICOMOS.

Barnett, Cherry. 1996. UNESCO's lifeline for Laos. *History Today* 46(4): 4–5.

Boccardi, Giovnni, and William Logan. 2007. *Reactive Monitoring Mission to the Town of Luang Prabang World Heritage Property Lao People's Democratic Republic.* Paris: UNESCO.

Boime, Albert. 1991. Patriarchy fixed in stone: Gutzon Borglum's "Mount Rushmore." *American Art* 5(1/2): 142–167.

Bruner, Edward M. 1996. Tourism in Ghana: Representations of slavery and the return of the Black Diaspora. *American Anthropologist* 98(2): 290–304.

Buzinde, Christine N. 2007. Representational politics of plantation heritage. In *Globalizing Cultural Studies,* C. McCarthy, A. Durham, E. L. A. Filmer, M. Giardina, and M. Malagreca, Eds., pp. 229–252. New York: Peter Lang Publishing.

Buzinde, Christine N., and Carla Almeida Santos. 2008. Representation of slavery. *Annals of Tourism Research* 35(2): 469–488.

Byrne, Denis. 2003. The ethos of return: Erasure and reinstatement of aboriginal visibility in the Australian historical landscape. *Historical Archaeology* 37(1): 73–86.

Center for Southeast Asian Studies. 2002. *The Pra Bang Image of the Buddha.* Dekalb: Northern Illinois University, www.seasite.niu.edu/lao/culture/LuangPrabang/PBimage.htm, accessed June 25, 2009.

Churchill, Winston. 1943. House of Commons (meeting in the House of Lords), 28 October.

Clarke, Annie, and Chris Johnston. 2003. Time, memory, place and land: Social meaning and heritage conservation in Australia. International Scientific Symposium "Place, memory, meaning: Preserving intangible values in monuments and sites," Victoria Falls, Zimbabwe. Vol. Sub Theme B, Section 3B. ICOMOS.

Connell, John, and Barbara Rugendyke. 2008. Tourism at the grassroots: Villagers and visitors in the Asia-Pacific, *Routledge Studies in Contemporary Geographies of Leisure, Tourism, and Mobility,* p. 1. London: Routledge.

Dann, Graham M. S., and A. V. Seaton. 2001. Slavery, contested heritage, and thanatourism. In *Slavery, Contested Heritage, and Thanatourism,* G. M. S. Dann and A. V. Seaton, Eds., pp. 1–29. Binghamton, NY: Haworth Press.

Di Giovine, Michael A. 2008. *The Heritage-Scape: UNESCO, World Heritage, and Tourism*. Lanham, MD: Lexington Books.

Dick, H. W., and P. J. Rimmer. 1998. Beyond the Third World city: The new urban geography of South-East Asia. *Urban Studies* 35(12): 2303–2321.

Dioko, Leonardo, and Tara Gujadhur. 2008. "Packaging" heritage for tourism: Modeling the effects on the practice and transmission of intangible heritage. In *Second International Colloquium on Tourism and Leisure*, M. Neal and C. Jones, Eds., pp. 67–76. Chiang Mai, Thailand: Balamand University.

Duke, Philip. 2007. *The Tourists Gaze, the Cretans Glance*. Walnut Creek, CA: Left Coast Press.

Essah, Patience. 2001. Slavery, heritage, and tourism in Ghana. In *Slavery, Contested Heritage, and Thanatourism*, G. M. S. Dann and A. V. Seaton, Eds., pp. 31–49. Binghamton, NY: Haworth Press.

Evans, G. 2002. *A Short History of Laos, the Land in Between*. Sydney: Allen & Unwin.

Fenelon, James V. 1997. From peripheral domination to internal colonialism: Socio-political change of the Lakota on Standing Rock. *Journal of World-Systems Research* 3: 259–320.

Fiji Islands Bureau of Statistics. 2007. Population Census. Suva: Fiji Islands Bureau of Statistics.

Graburn, Nelson H. H. 1977. Tourism: The sacred journey. In *Hosts and Guests*. V. L. Smith, Ed. Philadelphia: University of Pennsylvania Press.

Hall, C. Michael. 2001. World heritage and tourism. *Tourism Recreation Research* 26(1): 1–3.

Handler, Richard, and Eric Gable. 1997. *The New History in an Old Museum*. Durham, NC: Duke University Press.

Harrison, David. 2005a. Contested narratives in the domain of World Heritage. In *Politics of World Heritage: Negotiating Tourism and Conservation*, D. Harrison and M. Hitchcock, Eds., pp. 1–10. Buffalo: Channel View Productions.

———. 2005b. Levuka, Fiji: Contested heritage? In *The Politics of World Heritage*. D. Harrison and M. Hitchcock, Eds., pp. 66–89. Buffalo: Channel View Publications.

Hewison, Robert. 1989. Heritage: An interpretation. In *Heritage Interpretation: The Natural and Built Environment*, D. Uzzell, Ed., pp. 15–23, Vol. 1. London: Belhaven.

Hobsbawm, Eric, and Terence Ranger, Eds. 1983. *The Invention of Tradition*. Cambridge: Cambridge University Press.

Ivarsson, Søren. 2008. *Creating Laos: The Making of a Lao Space between Indochina and Siam, 1860–1945*. Copenhagen: NIAS Press.

Jerndal, Randi, and Janothan Rigg. 1999. From buffer state to crossroads state. In *Laos: Culture and Soceity*, G. Evans, Ed. Chiang Mai: Silkworm.

Kirshenblatt-Gimblett, Barbara. 1995. Theorizing heritage. *Ethnomusicology* 39(3): 14.

Kostoff, Spiro. 1991. *The City Shaped: Urban Patterns and Meanings through History*, p. 10. London: Thames and Hudson.

La Maison du Patrimoine. 2001. *Heritage Preservation and Development Plan*. Luang Prabang: La Maison du Patrimoine.

Lal, Brij V. 2000a. *Chalo Jahaji: On a Journey through Indenture in Fiji*. Canberra: Australian National University and Fiji Museum.

———. 2000b. Madness in May: George Speight and the unmaking of modern Fiji. In *Before the Storm: Elections and Politics of Development*, B. V. Lal, Ed., pp. 175–194. Canberra: Asia-Pacific Press at the Australian National University.

LeBar, Frank M., and Adrienne Suddard. 1967. *Laos, Its People, Its Society, Its Culture: Survey of World Cultures*, Vol. 8. New Haven, CT: Hraf Press.

Lee, Lik Meng, Yoke Mui Lim, and Yusuf Nor'Aini. 2008. Strategies for urban conservation: A case example of George Town, Penang. *Habitat International* 32(3): 293–304.

Lieberman, Victor. 2003. *Strange Parallels: South Asia in Global Context, c. 800–1830*, Vol. 1: *Integration on the Mainland*. Cambridge: Cambridge University Press.

Ling, Ooi Giok, and Brian J. Shaw. 2009. Paradise lost? Islands, global tourism and heritage erasure in Malaysia and Singapore. In *Southeast Asian Culture and Heritage in a Globalising World*, R. Ismail, B. J. Shaw, and O. G. Ling, Eds., pp. 43–58. Farnham, Surrey: Ashgate Publishing Limited.

Long, Colin. 2003. The persistance of tradition in Laos. In *Asia's Old Dwellings*, R. G. Knapp, Ed., pp. 185–202. New York: Oxford University Press.

Long, Colin, and Jonathan Sweet. 2006. Globalization, nationalism and World Heritage: Interpreting Luang Prabang. *South East Asia Research* 14(3): 445–469.

Lowenthal, David. 1986. *The Past Is a Foreign Country*. Cambridge: Cambridge University Press.

———. 1998. Fabricating heritage. *History & Memory* 10(1): 5–24.

McGuire, Randall H. 1992. Archeology and the First Americans. *American Anthropologist* 94(4): 816–836.

Ministry of Information and Culture—Lao PDR. 2003a. *Periodic Reporting Exercise on the Application of the World Heritage Convention. Section I: Application of the World Heritage Convention by the State Party,* D.o.M.a. Archeology, Ed. Vientiane: UNESCO.

———. 2003b. *Periodic Reporting Exercise on the Application of the World Heritage Convention. Section II: State of Conservation of Specific World Heritage Properties,* D.o.M.a. Archeology, Ed. Vientiane: UNESCO.

Mohamed, Badaruddin, A. Ghafar Ahmad, and Izzamr Ismail. 2001. Heritage routes along ethnic lines: The case of Penang. In *Making Tracks*. Alice Springs: Australia ICOMOS.

Mohamed, Badaruddin, and Rahmat Azam Mustafa. 2003. *Heritage Tourism in a Multicultural Society: The Case of Malaysia.* The 3rd Global Summit on Peace Through Tourism—Education Forum, Pattaya, Thailand, 2003, pp. 141–147. International Forum for Peace Through Tourism.

Mooney, Barbara Burlison. 2004. Looking for history's huts. *Winterthur Portfolio* 39(1): 43–68.

Mumford, Lewis. 1989. *The City in History: Its Origins, Its Transformations, and Its Prospects,* p. 569. New York: Harcourt Brace.

Paulsson, Urban. 2008. *Mekong Riverview Hotel, Luang Prabang, Lao PDR* www.mekongriverview.com/pages/rooms.htm, accessed January 26, 2010.

Pretes, Michael. 2003. Tourism and nationalism. *Annals of Tourism Research* 30(1): 125–142.

Rakic, Tijana. 2007. World heritage: Issues and debates. *Tourism: An International Interdisciplinary Journal* 55(2): 209–219.

Rakic, Tijana, and Donna Chambers. 2008. World heritage: Exploring the tension between the national and the "universal." *Journal of Heritage Tourism* 3(2): 145–160.

Rehbein, Bioke. 2007. *Globalization, Culture and Society in Laos.* New York: Routledge.

Richards, Sandra L. 2002. Cultural travel to Ghana's slave castles: A commentary. *International Research in Geographical and Environmental Education* 11(4): 372–375.

Richter, Linda K. 1989. *The Politics of Tourism in Asia.* Honolulu: University of Hawaii Press.

Rigg, Jonathan. 2005. *Living with Transition in Laos: Market Integration in Southeast Asia.* London: Routledge.

Savada, Andrea Matles, Ed. 1995. *Laos: A Country Study.* Washington D.C.: Federal Research Division Library of Congress.

Scully, Vincent. 1988. *American Architecture and Urbanism*, p. 203. Henry Holt and co.

Seaton, A. V. 2001. Sources of slavery: Destinations of slavery. In *Slavery, Contested Heritage and Thanatourism.* G. M. S. Dann and A. V. Seaton, Eds., pp. 107–129. Binghamton, NY: Haworth Press.

Shackley, Myra. 2001. Potential future for Robben Island. *International Journal of Heritage Studies* 7(4): 355–363.

Slatyer, Ralph O. 1983a. How the World Heritage Convention works. *Ambio* 12(3/4): 140–145.

———. 1983b. The origin and evolution of the World Heirtage Convention. *Ambio* 12(3/4): 138–140.

Smith, Laurajane. 2007. Empty gestures? Heritage and the politics of recognition. In *Cultural Heritage and Human Rights*, H. Silverman and D. F. Ruggles, Eds. New York: Springer.

Socio-Economic & Environmental Research Institute. 2002. *Population and Housing Census of Malaysia 2000.* Department of Statistics, Ed. Penang: Penang State Government.

Stuart-Fox, Martin. 1983. Marxism and Theravada Buddhism: The legitimation of political authority in Laos. *Political Affairs* 56(3): 428–454.

———. 1996. *Buddhist Kingdom, Marxist State: The Making of Modern Laos.* Bangkok: White Lotus.

———. 1997. *A History of Laos.* Cambridge: Cambridge University Press.

Tagore, Rabindranath, and Rabindra-Rachanabali. 1939. *Collected Works of Rabindranath Tagore,* Vol. I, p. 1. Calcutta: Visva-Bharati.

Teo, Peggy. 2003. The limits of imagineering: A case study of Penang. *International Journal of Urban and Regional Research* 27(3): 545–563.

Thorley, Peter. 2002. Current realities, idealised pasts: Archaeology, values, and indigenous heritage management in central Australia. *Oceania* 73: 110–125.

Titchen, Sarah M. 1996. On the construction of "Outstanding Universal Value." *Conservation and Management of Archaeological Sites* 1(4): 235–242.

Travers, Robert. 2007. Economic corridors and ecotourism: Whither tourism in Laos? In *Asian Tourism: Growth and Change.* J. Cochrane, Ed., pp. 105–116. London: Elsevier.

Tunbridge, John E., and Gregory J. Ashworth. 1996. *Dissonant Heritage: The Management of the Past as a Resource in Conflict.* Chichester: Wiley.

Turtinen, Jan. 2000. *Globalising Heritage: On UNESCO and the Transnational Construction of a World Heritage.* Stockholm: Stockholm Center for Organizational Research.

UNESCO. 1972. *Convention Concerning the Protection of the World Cultural and Natural Heritage.* Paris: UNESCO.

———. 1995. *UNESCO World Heritage Committee Nineteenth Session.* Paris: UNESCO.

———. 1998. *Convention Concerning the Protection of the World Cultural and Natural Heritage,* Twenty-second Session. Kyoto, Japan.

———. 2003. *Convention for the Safeguarding of the Intangible Cultural Heritage.* Paris: UNESCO.

———. 2004. *Impact: The Effects of Tourism on Culture and the Environment in Asia and the Pacific: Tourism and Heritage Site Management in Luang Prabang, Lao PDR.* Bangkok: Office of the Regional Advisor for Culture in

Asia and the Pacific, UNESCO Bangkok; Manoa: School of Travel Industry Management, University of Hawai'i.

———. 2009a. *About World Heritage*. Paris: UNESCO World Heritage Centre. http://whc.unesco.org/en/about/, accessed January 26, 2010.

———. 2009b. *The Convention: Brief History*, Paris: UNESCO Cultural Heritage Centre. http://whc.unesco.org/en/convention/, accessed January 26, 2010.

———. 2009c. *World Heritage, The List*, Paris: UNESCO World Heritage Centre. http://whc.unesco.org/en/list/34/, accessed January 26, 2010.

UNWTO. 1994. Recommendations on tourism statistics. In *Statistical Papers. Series M.* Madrid.

Urry, John. 2002. *The Tourist Gaze*. London: SAGE.

Uzzell, David. 1989a. *Heritage Interpretation: The Natural and Built Environment* (2 vols.). Vol. 1. London: Belhaven.

———. 1989b. *Heritage Interpretation: The Visitor Experience* (2 vols.). Vol. 2. London: Belhaven.

Watkins, Joe Edward. 2006. *Sacred Sites and Repatriation*. New York: Chelsea House Publishers.

Williams, Anthony V., and Wilbur Zelinsky. 1970. On some patterns in international tourist flows. *Economic Geography* 46(4): 549–567.

Wolters, O. W. 1982. *History, Culture and Region in Southeast Asian Perspectives*. Singapore: Institute of Southeast Asian Studies.

World Heritage Committee. 2008. *Decisions Report of the 32nd Session*, pp. 105–106. Quebec: UNESCO.

GLOSSARY

ban	Lao word meaning "village."
binthabat	Morning alms-giving by residents to monks and novices as a way of earning merit.
Buddha	Refers to the historical Buddha, the founder of Buddhism (known as Shakyamuni Buddha), who was born approximately 2,300 years ago in present-day Nepal. The term Buddha is also used to refer to anyone who has attained full enlightenment, who

has awakened from the sleep of ignorance, and sees things as they really are.

Fa Ngum   The king who unified Laos in 1353.

heritage interpretation   A particular reading or explanation about the nature, importance, and purpose of historical, natural, or cultural resources in order to facilitate understanding of particular significant objects, sites, and phenomena.

Heuanchan   Lao word meaning "Moon House"; in Luang Prabang this refers to the facilities of La Maison du Patrimoine, established as a tourist center.

La Maison du Patrimoine   French for "Heritage House."

LPDR   Lao Peoples Democratic Republic

mandala   Historical political formation of Southeast Asia of variable geometry where subordinate powers may belong to and pay tribute to several mandalas.

meuang   Subordinate power that falls under the influence of one or more mandalas.

Mount Phousi   Locally sacred hill in the middle of the Luang Prabang peninsula that houses several Buddhist shrines.

naga   A deity that takes the form of a hooded serpent.

phi	A local protective spirit.
Pra Bang	Particular Buddha statue that is the palladium and protectorate of the royal family of Luang Prabang. Fa Ngum brought the statue to Luang Prabang in 1359 as a gift from his father-in-law, the Khmer King of Angkor.
Sangha	The community of ordained Buddhist monks.
stupa	A mound-shaped monument built to hold sacred relics or ashes of abbots, monks, or other devout Buddhists.
that	Laotian for *stupa*.
torchis	A building technique similar to wattle and daub, with bamboo strips as the substrate.
UNESCO	United Nations Educational, Scientific, and Cultural Organization.
wat	Buddhist monastery/temple complex.

INDEX

Note: Page numbers in italics indicate illustrations.

delisting of World Heritage Sites, 141, 144
Duke, Phillip, 135

Eastern and Orient Hotel, Georgetown, 43
economics of heritage, 20, 109, 138, 140
Elmina Castle, Ghana, 35–36
emendments
> of buildings classified for preservation and restoration, 100
> as companion to the manufacture of heritage, 28
> in packaging Luang Prabang's heritage as World Heritage, 63
> physical, and erasure, 49
> of physical and cultural heritage, in Georgetown, 41–42
> in production of heritage, 33–34
> in recreation of an imagined colonial past, 128–30
> targeted, as element of World Heritage designation process, 26, 27
> in the urban environment, 124

erasures
> black-coded buildings and, 124
> of buildings classified for preservation and restoration, 105
> the Heuanchan Complex and, 115
> of the inconvenient, 34
> of indigenous groups in United States and Australia, 46–48
> of inequalities, 44
> interpretations of heritage and, 28–30
> of meaning in lives of Penang's residents, 42
> physical, and expunction of social structure, 43
> of the politically inexpedient, 45–48

of the real world, 128
sites of, in Luang Prabang, 93, *94*
of village life, 102
of white-coded buildings, 112

Fa Ngum, 54
Fiji, 38, 39–40, 140
"Four Thieves" (Mount Rushmore), 48
French colonialism
> and influences on built environment, 71, 75–77, 81–82
> in Laos, 57–59
> and Mandala-Muang structure, 56
French Laos, 57–58

Georgetown, Panang, 41–44
Ghana, coastal castles of, 35–36, 59
global flows, 132–34
globalization, 132
Greck, François, 133
guesthouse landscapes, 124–27
guesthouses
> in Ban Houaxieng, 124
> in Ban Khili, 97, *98, 99*, 100
> in Ban Vatthat, 124, *125*
> on main road, 112
> on north peninsula, 93

Harrison, D., 23, 132
heritage
> authenticity vs. integrity in evaluation of, 27
> built environments as focus of interpretations of, 26, 29–30
> contested nature of, 28–30, 36, 48
> cultural, 18–19
> defined, 16–17
> economics of, 20, 109, 138, 140
> emending, in production of, 33–34

ABOUT THE AUTHORS

Lynne M. Dearborn is an Assistant Professor of Architecture and Urban Planning at the University of Illinois at Urbana-Champaign, where she teaches design studios and community-based design seminars. Professor Dearborn's research interests focus on the nexus of culture and the built environment. She is particularly interested in the relationship between planning and the physical outcomes of architecture and their impact on marginalized and underserved communities. She received her Ph.D. in Architecture from the University of Wisconsin, Milwaukee, in 2004.

John C. Stallmeyer is an Assistant Professor of Architecture at the University of Illinois at Urbana-Champaign, where he teaches design studios, research methods courses, and seminars examining the influence of globalization on the built environment. Professor Stallmeyer's research interests address the influence of global processes on architecture and urban production. His focus is how globally transmitted imagery and ideas influence the production of built space. He received his Ph.D. in Architecture from the University of California, Berkeley, in 2006.